This book is presented to you
by

A. E. LePAGE

in recognition of
Calgary's Centennial, 1984

CALGARY
100
1884 - 1984

CALGARY
A Living Heritage

EDITED BY SUSIE SPARKS
PUBLISHED BY THE JUNIOR LEAGUE OF CALGARY

For information about this book, or to order copies,
please contact The Junior League of Calgary, or
the Glenbow Museum Shop, Glenbow Museum,
130 9 Avenue S.E., Calgary, Alberta, T2G 0P3.

Printed and bound in Canada

Contents

From the Mayor's Office

It is an honour to include my good wishes in The Junior League of Calgary's new book, *Calgary: A Living Heritage*.

1984 marks Calgary's centennial of incorporation, and what better way to pay tribute to our founding fathers than by the publication of this commemorative book.

I commend The Junior League of Calgary for the initiative and creativity they have displayed in compiling this landmark publication.

Ralph Klein
MAYOR, The City of Calgary

Acknowledgements

In 1980 the Junior League of Calgary made a formal commitment to aid in the preservation of the city's historical resources. Projects partially funded and staffed by League volunteers have included the Stephen Avenue Walking and Armchair Tours, a Driving Tour, identification plaques for historic buildings, the Glenbow Archives Oral Histories Project, and the restoration of the Deane House.

Volunteers involved with these projects had an invaluable opportunity to get to know the personality behind Calgary's pioneer architecture. They recognized that memoirs and anecdotes were as endangered as the old sandstone that weathers away with time, and that an effort should be made to preserve those stories as well. And so, it was to this end that *Calgary: A Living Heritage* was published.

Although it was never the intention to prepare a documented historical account, it was agreed that these personal reminiscences contained the flavour, if not the substance, of history. Every effort was made, therefore, to publish a variety of interesting vignettes culled from family journals, diaries, oral histories and written memoirs. Family photo albums were generously shared with the publishing committee and more stories came to light as more long-forgotten memories were recalled.

Unhappily, space did not permit publication of every wonderful anecdote, and the task of selecting among them was a difficult one indeed. Above all, the Junior League of Calgary would like to thank each talented writer who submitted material for the book. We would also like to acknowledge the many people whose dedication and encouragement assisted us throughout the compilation of this volume:

Susie Sparks: *editor*
Rick Budd: *graphic designer*
David Scollard and Rose Veighey: *production supervisors*
Dennis Budgen: *cover artist*
Mr. D. Newton: *cover design subject matter*
Georgeen Klassen and the Glenbow Archives staff: *historic photographs*
Crowchild Photography Ltd.: *biography photographs*
Nina Kilpatrick and Susan Williams: *Chairmen of The Junior League Heritage Book Committee*

Financial assistance from the following sources is gratefully acknowledged:

Alberta Culture
The Allstate Foundation of Canada
The Devonian Group of Charitable Foundations

Active and sustaining members of The Junior League of Calgary who volunteered their time and enthusiasm to make this volume a reality:

Active Members

Nancy Blue
Nancy Cadwallader
Laurel Chrumka
Marcia Clark
Patricia Cooper
Patti Culver
Marnie Dabbs
Stephanie Felesky
Charlotte Firth
Judy Gorkoff
Christy Holdsworth
Rosemary Jonassen
Lynne Kennedy
Carol Kiernan
Nina Kilpatrick
Flo Lampard
Dorie Legat
Joy Long
Carol Mahan
Karen Marks
Bambi Morton
Heide Neth-Hoelzel
Sheila Padley
Martha Parker
Dianne Porteous
Kathryn Plumb
Glenda Waddingham
Susan Williams
Florin Wolfer

Sustaining Members

Gail Beaumont
Gail Einer
Marilyn Jermyn
Patricia McCaffery
Pat Pryde
Ruth Sherwood
Helen Thomson
Helen Wells

THE JUNIOR LEAGUE OF CALGARY

The purpose of The Junior League is exclusively educational and charitable; its aim is to promote voluntarism, to develop the potential of its members for voluntary participation in community affairs, and to demonstrate the effectiveness of trained volunteers. The profit realized by The Junior League of Calgary from the sale of this book will be used to support community projects that we undertake. It is to this community in its centennial year, and the memories of the men and women of Calgary's past, that we proudly dedicate this book.

Lynne Kennedy
President
The Junior League of Calgary

Preface

The young man, who had only the day before alighted from the westbound CPR, rose early. He was wakened by the breakfast smells that lingered on the Indian summer breeze, and turned toward the open window of his room. A low murmur of voices in the street outside beckoned his attention and, as he quickly slipped back into his train-rumpled clothes, he edged closer to the conversation outside.

The cluster of men gathered outside the Grand Central Hotel had, by this time, rehashed all the old arguments too many times to count, so the telegraphed news seemed vaguely anticlimactic. Heads down, hands thrust deep in pockets, scuffing little clouds of dust as their circle shifted slightly to include the newcomer, they scarcely acknowledged his presence, and their conversation continued around him. But since he was uninvolved in the political manoeuvres of the previous ten months, the young man soon lost interest and wandered toward the high ground that overlooked the little community. As he paused in his climb through the autumn-dried grass, he discovered a panoramic view of the two rivers merging below him, the fort at their junction, with the stretch of sun-glinted peaks to the west.

It was mid-November, 1884.

That young man was barely twenty-two years old. The little prairie town below him was brand new. Perhaps the news of the town's incorporation was guardedly welcomed by its pioneers, but he, for one, regarded it as an omen full of bright optimism. Together they couldn't fail.

More sober-headed citizens, however, had reason for skepticism, and older and wiser immigrants to this far West knew only too well the hardships that lay ahead. Coming to the Territories had been, for the most, no spur-of-the-moment lark. There were those who had uprooted their families from deeply entrenched eastern comforts to pit their fortunes on little more than a gamble. That the CPR changed its route in 1882 to travel west through the Bow Valley was the greatest good fortune for those first settlers, and they congratulated themselves on their foresight. But even though they could at last look forward to some far distant prosperity, hard reality loomed anew each day.

Despite the bountiful promises of CPR advertisements, life was tough where nature provided few bonuses. There were no trees; lumber for housing had to be floated down the Bow from the distant forests of the foothills. Winters were cold, and, even with the brief chinook respites, the season dragged on for interminable months. Spring thaws and rains brought the annual floods that made dirt streets quagmires of muck, and summer heat and dust storms plagued the overworked women to the point that many cracked from the strain.

Some retreated to the paved, tree-shaded neighbourhoods of their home towns back East, where lamp lights glowed after dark and trolley cars whisked theatre patrons to bustling, fashionable city centres. There was nothing glamorous about life on the frontier and it took strong stuff to survive the western community's growing pains.

That first excited flush of debate over the town's incorporation had been tempered by an economic downturn, so that, by October, many Calgarians were arguing that municipal status would only necessitate burdensome taxes, and even the usually effervescent *Calgary Herald* admitted that civic improvements could mean heavy monetary outlays. But the gamble was made — tentatively by many, wholeheartedly by some — and all settled in for the long haul toward the twentieth century.

Fortunately for the little town, the men and women who stayed, and those who came along after them, were, for the most part, those naturally selected by the frontiering spirit. They were, by character, the less cautious of their eastern contemporaries. They were, primarily, the middle class whose drive for self-improvement gave them an inherently progressive spirit, and their optimism carried them through their years of deprivation.

That same spirit, however, would conspire against them as the new century at first brought rapid growth and prosperity, followed only by war, drought and depression. Even in 1884 the *Herald* had warned: "If Regina is going to send delegates from the North-West Territories to Ottawa we might very well join them and have a representation of our own. If our rulers, for unhappily we are not permitted to rule ourselves, are kindly disposed to us, now is the time to strengthen their hands. If the reverse is the case, now is the time to make them show their hands — whichever it be. Alberta will never come to the fore unless it unites in an effort."

But it was difficult for these fiercely proud and independent Albertans to admit to forces beyond their control. Political power was dispersed horizontally here on the prairies, and women gained a political voice almost as quickly as the ordinary rank-and-file farmer and townsman. And the farmers' movement of the 1920s, followed by the Social Credit Party of the '30s, illustrated just how plastic and independent of federal influences the political milieu was. Even though Albertans suffered worse than most during the desperately hard Depression era, and sacrificed their youngest and strongest to the war years, they survived — convinced again that their fate lay in their own hands.

And so it happened that that young fellow who stepped from the train onto the dusty street of 1884 would live long enough to take his place in the growing community, and would ride out the difficult years in anticipation of better times. He was an old man, though, by 1950 — by the time Calgary began a boom unparalleled since the early years of the century. He would not live to see his great-grandchild make her contribution to Calgary's development as a major Canadian city, and so it is his story that we share and applaud — his and the countless other individuals whose stories here thread through the fabric of our history. Without them, without their humour and self-deprecating tales of tenacity and triumph, we would not be who we are today. To them — to that young man smiling down upon the vista that lay below him that November day a hundred years ago — we dedicate this book.

Susie Sparks, editor
Autumn, 1984

The First Big Drive

by Tom Moore

Tom Moore emigrated from Ireland with his parents at an early age. He attended public school and SAIT in Calgary, and interested in writing, became a protégé of Everett Marshall, managing editor of the Herald. *Mr. Moore began his lifetime career with the* Albertan *as a sports writer and sports editor, later becoming police and political reporter, city and news editor, editorial writer and columnist, and finally managing editor.*

In writing a special seventy-fifth anniversary edition of the Albertan, *Moore researched local history personally through the city's legendary old-timers, and it is a selection of those stories that appears in this volume.*

Now retired, Mr. Moore volunteers for the Kerby Centre, the Alberta Council on Aging, and helps senior citizens write their life stories for the benefit of future generations.

Mewata Park in Calgary has seen just about everything. Site of the big brick armouries from which Calgary soldiers marched to two world wars, it has also housed Mewata Stadium in which some of the West's greatest gridiron games were played before McMahon Stadium came into being in northwest Calgary. It was at one time the city's finest baseball diamond. It was the range over which local shotgun artists tested their skill; it was the location of a big Vienna-style skating rink and several hockey rinks. It was the scene of hundreds of high school and other major track meets; site of unnumbered Scottish Games and dancing competitions; the place where Stampede barbecues and all sorts of band concerts and competitions have drawn spectators whose aggregate numbers over the years must run into the millions, so it most certainly has lived up to its Indian name, roughly translated as "to be happy".

But, before all the other events crowded into its tight boundaries, it was the scene of an event that was both tragic and historic — a scene that opened a major chapter in the industry with which Calgary has always been associated — cattle ranching.

Only five years after the first herd of range cattle — twenty-one cows and a bull — had been brought to the Calgary district from Montana by H.A. "Fred" Kanouse, the famous Cochrane Ranche Company went "big time" on the cattle trail. The company bought between six and seven thousand head from the I.G. Baker Company in Montana, whose men were to deliver them to the ranch west of Calgary. Howell Harris and Frank Strong were in charge of the drive, with thirty cowboys and three hundred horses handling the gigantic herd.

The herd moved north in two groups — steers in one, cows and calves in the other, and movement was made at a killing pace. Steers averaged fifteen to eighteen miles per day. Cows and their calves were sometimes forced to cover fourteen miles. A number of wagons trailed along behind to pick up calves too weak to survive the march, but hundreds perished on the trail. Never before, or since, had such numbers of cattle been moved so rapidly over so great a distance. It was a herd of worn and weary stock that was finally turned over to Major James Walker, manager of the Cochrane spread, at what is now Mewata Park.

From there they were driven west to their new range — but the ordeal was not over. An early winter gave them no chance to recover from the gruelling trek from Montana and hundreds died before they could find shelter and water. When spring finally broke, the Bow Valley was strewn with the carcasses of the Cochrane herd. It was a stiff blow to the infant cattle industry, and when more tragedy struck the Cochrane herd in the winter of 1882-'83, it is a wonder that the early pioneers didn't give up and abandon the trade that was later to make Calgary famous as the greatest "cowtown" of the Canadian West.

Right: *Howell Harris, included in this 1901 round-up photo, was a veteran of the first major cattle drive from Montana into the Calgary District. Never before, or since, had such numbers of cattle been moved so rapidly over so great a distance.*

Below: *Even after the cattle industry was well established in Alberta, range herds were at the mercy of erratic prairie weather. Freak blizzards dealt killing blows to spring calves too young to survive such onslaughts.*

In the summer of '82, the Cochrane Ranche purchased about five thousand head from the Poindexter and Orr Company of Montana and trekked them overland to the ranch. This time the cattle ran into an early October blizzard. The weary cattle were driven fast but could find no feed. A thaw followed. Then came more bitter cold, freezing the surface of the snow into a hard crust. Again, cattle by the hundreds perished.

But the Cochrane outfit, which had as a bookkeeper A.E. Cross (who was later to become founder of the Calgary Brewery), was undaunted. They persisted in raising cattle, and business was expanded to include an immense tract of land in the Cardston district. It observedly prospered, and things improved on the range closer to Calgary as well.

Other ranches in Southern Alberta had their troubles, too – the Quorn, the Oxley, the Bar U, the Critchley, the Halifax, the Bow Valley, the Flying E, the Waldron and all the others – but they managed to survive and then expand. And, with the expansion, Calgary became centre of the industry and earned the name by which it will always be affectionately known wherever cattlemen gather – the "Cowtown" of the West.

They hand-picked for the job men of superb physique, men who could stand long hours in open weather, men who could rough it in the toughest sense of the word. Not just a few men, but splendid physical specimens by the hundreds.

The front train's two engines pulled a mile of steel: six cars of rails, ten cars of ties, two cars of bridge timbers, two cars of telegraph poles, boarding cars and sleeping cars.

18

Bringing the Steel to Calgary

by Tom Moore

Talk about "teams" and the strong young men who belong to them, and it's natural to think of football, hockey or other sports which have provided athletic entertainment over the years. Calgary has had its share of great ones, but probably the greatest team of all, the finest collection of co-ordinated muscle-power ever seen in the West, a record-breaking crew whose exploits were reported around the world, had nothing to do with sport.

That team was the Langdon and Shepard construction gang that brought the railroad into Calgary in August of 1883 after the greatest track-laying drive in all history.

Langdon was a stonemason of Scottish descent, Shepard an engineer, (their names are perpetuated today by small towns just east of Calgary), and they had the CPR construction contract for the prairies.

They hand-picked for the job men of superb physique, men who could stand long hours in open weather, men who could rough it in the toughest sense of the word. Not just a few men, but splendid physical specimens by the hundreds. Men such as the Ryan brothers, world's champion spikers, who could sink a railroad spike with two blows. Men such as engineers Jim O'Hagan and Leslie McLaughlin and firemen "Scotty" Ormiston and William Pullar, who could work sixteen hours a day on the engines of the "front" train and make their own repairs along the way. Men who could co-ordinate their own muscle power with superb timing, men who could rise to the challenge of construction boss Donald Grant as he fought against time and set track-laying records along the way. Men who were really men.

Scores of grading and surveying camps were strung out across the prairies as the thin bands of steel stretched into the west. Activity centred on the "front train" — the train that "never went back" except to the nearest siding to pick up more supplies. The front train's two engines pulled a mile of steel: six cars of rails, ten cars of ties, two cars of bridge timbers, two cars of telegraph poles, boarding cars and sleeping cars.

Temporary camp was made during the summer of '83 at the end of the line, where bone-weary men rested for each new attempt at a track-laying record.

19

Langdon and Shepard, realizing that the strongest of men must be healthy if they are to achieve great feats of endurance and strength, did not spare expense in providing supplies. It took that, plus the superb teamwork to set the records that brought the steel into Calgary.

When the front train pushed to the end of the rails, about thirty-five teams of horses hauled railway ties ahead, placing them in position on the grade. Rails, loaded on a truck hauled by two horses, moved forward. Six men on each side of the track pulled rails from the truck over a roller at the front end, and placed them in position. Two gaugers lined them up, four men with crowbars braced the ties at each end, four others set fishplates into position and four spikers hammered the spikes home. The rail car rolled ahead to repeat the routine while the rest of the gang moved up to spike the lines of steel to the rest of the ties. It was a steady grind, but it made steady progress.

A total of four hundred forty-five miles of steel had been laid west of Winnipeg in 1882

By August of 1883, the steel reached Calgary and opened the West to the waves of immigration that would

before winter halted construction, with the rails going down at an average of three to four miles per day. Work resumed the next spring.

In July of 1883, the front train was west of Medicine Hat. The tempo stepped up. Between Cassils and Southesk, on July 7, a record of six miles of rail was laid in ninety degree heat. But Donald Grant, looking ahead, still saw the need for fighting time. He scheduled his onslaught on the record for July 28. Langdon and Shepard's company forces anticipated a record-breaking distance of nine miles, but, despite a feverish attempt, the crew was only successful in beating their previous record by half a mile — still a respectable distance and the track-laying record for the entire transcontinental project.

From that point, near Strathmore, it was only a step to Calgary — end of the Langdon and Shepard contract. But it was also a beginning — the beginning of the metamorphosis of the quiet NWMP post and village into the bustling metropolis that the Foothills City has since become.

transform the quiet NWMP post to a bustling metropolis of the twentieth century.

J.W. Costello: Patriarch of the Calgary Clan

by Sam McDonald

Sam McDonald is the grandson of one of Calgary's most famous pioneers, J. W. Costello. He tells about the family — its successes and hardships alike — with the immediacy of a real participant in Calgary's history. With the exception of a five year stint in the army overseas, Mr. McDonald has been a lifelong Calgarian, and, for over twenty-five years, has been in the service station business.

My grandfather, John William Costello, was born in 1842, a good Irish Catholic who, like so many others, fell victim of the hard times in the old country and emigrated as a young man to the Ottawa Valley in about 1860. There he met and married the Irish girl who would become mother of his six children and matriarch of the Calgary clan of Costellos. Their story, while typical of so many pioneers, is particularly significant to western history, and I have always had a great deal of pride in being part of it.

Papa Costello, although settled for many years in Ontario with a growing family, felt again the urge to seek out new opportunities, and went west in June of 1883. When he arrived in Calgary he discovered a community of about two hundred hearty souls, like himself, eager to be part of an exciting new era. He was confident in the future of the new community, so he immediately turned around to conclude his affairs in the East, collect his brood and prepare for the new life that awaited in the Territories.

Less than three months later Papa, Nana and their five children boarded the first passenger train and arrived in Calgary in August, 1883. My mother, Molly Costello, was the eighteen-month-old toddler of the family and her younger sister, Lilly, who would be born four months later, was the first white girl born in Calgary. Papa quickly found work with a company that sold supplies to the railway workers. (Calgary was the CPR construction base for the track that was being laid from the east into the mountains.)

Within a year the little community had grown so rapidly that municipal status was attained, and it was incumbent upon the new Council to provide a school. Since Papa Costello

The Costello family, arriving in Calgary on the first passenger train in 1883, grew and thrived with the little town. John Costello, seated right.

had a teacher's certificate, he was hired at fifty dollars a month to teach the twelve children. But, by the time the school year ended, thirty-eight more students had joined the little school and Grandfather decided to retire to less taxing responsibilities. Even though he then took a permanent job with the Federal Government as Inspector of Weights and Measures, he maintained his interest in education and was a member of the School Board, a long-standing commitment he made to the new community.

The family prospered along with the village and was able to move into a house on Fourth Street West between Seventh and Eighth Avenues South. By 1910 the burgeoning real estate market had attracted J.W.'s attention and he associated himself with the builders of the day. He was able then to move into the big brick house in Rouleauville — now the Mission District — the centre of Calgary's Catholic population, and, during the next few years, built five more homes for his children. The Catholic community thrived with developing Calgary, and Papa, who took his religion seriously and was a great friend of Father Lacombe, was instrumental in building the Holy Cross Hospital. The family still treasures the relic of the saints that was given to my grandparents by the Grey Nuns in appreciation of their generosity.

Papa Costello died in 1918, an old man of seventy-six who had lived a full and rewarding life. His three sons honoured his memory by their continuing commitment to his adopted home; Mike served three terms as Mayor of Calgary from 1915 to 1918, and Tom became one of the town's first doctors. All six children had married before his death and between them produced nineteen grandchildren. His legacy to this fine family was his unshakable faith in the opportunities that Calgary offered. He saw that little community of two hundred grow during his lifetime to a thriving city of seventy thousand, so I doubt that he would be surprised to know that by 1983 his little clan numbered 319 descendants.

Calgary's Debt to a Bucking Horse

by Grant MacEwan

Grant MacEwan has had a long and distinguished career as historian, journalist, author, lecturer, teacher, agriculturalist, politician and public servant in western Canada.

Dr. MacEwan was born in Manitoba in 1902, the son of pioneer prairie farmers, and from his early years gained a true appreciation and knowledge of the development of agriculture in the West. In

1962 he was appointed Lieutenant-Governor of Alberta, an honour which has been followed by many others, including honorary degrees from the universities of Alberta, Calgary, Saskatchewan, Guelph and Brandon. But perhaps even more important is the affection conferred upon him by his fellow citizens who, like his countless students and his reading public, know Grant MacEwan to be a man of warm humour and great kindness.

Horses played a big part in the life of Calgary, and Calgarians had their favourites: the stout-hearted little thoroughbred, Joey, at his death was buried reverently at Victoria Park; Bara Lad, owned by Peter Welsh, was the winner of the 1925 world's high jump record of eight feet, one and one-half inches; and Rex Stonewall was the proud leader of Calgary's most important parades for many years. To that honoured list should be appended the name of another horse but unfortunately his name is not known. All we know is that he was involved in one of the biggest real estate transactions of the last century, and the debt Calgary owes him continues to this day. The circumstances are unusual enough to be worthy of record.

Fate's involvement in the case began in 1884 or 1885, soon after early Calgary citizens met to organize the Agricultural Society which was to be the forerunner of the internationally famous Calgary Exhibition and Stampede. For reasons best known to the directors, no fair was held in either of the first two years, but the fair of 1886 was sufficiently successful to make its officers wish for a fair ground to which they would have exclusive claim. Claxton's Star Rink and the open space around it was all right for the first fair, but if non-paying guests were to be exclud-

The Calgary Exhibition became a grand annual attraction once a permanent home was found. Victoria Park was purchased by the Calgary Agricultural Society for two dollars and fifty cents an acre.

ed, something with a tight fence would be needed. Major James Walker, formerly of the Northwest Mounted Police, was, as president of the Agricultural Society, well aware of the need for a tract of land for a permanent home for an annual fair.

As it happened, A.M. Burgess, Deputy Minister of the Interior, came from Ottawa to inspect some Crown Land in the vicinity of Fish Creek. To carry out his task, he borrowed a horse and saddle and blithely rode away southward. The morning, we may presume, was bright and the mountains stood out with majestic clearness. The eastern man probably regretted the necessity of having to return to Ottawa, but his joy was too good to last, and, for reasons never to be explained, the Deputy Minister's un-named horse, which had begun the day like a gentle old school pony, chose an isolated stretch of grass near the creek to perform some cowcountry tricks. Perhaps his point was to remind the civil servant that life consists of more than carefree riding on a summer morning. In any case, the bronco launched into a display of fancy bucking, and the unsuspecting Deputy Minister bounced high in the air. When the rider came down the nameless horse was long gone. The result was a fractured collarbone and a severe bruise to eastern pride.

That much was entirely understandable. Eastern Deputy Ministers riding western horses with ranch antecedents might have expected as much. But what was particularly remarkable was that James Walker, president of the Agricultural Society, was driving that way with a team and

26

The Midway, 1908.

wagon, almost as though he had anticipated something of consequence, and, like the Good Samaritan of old, promptly rescued the injured man and took him to the Walker home to rest and convalesce.

Nobody suggested that Walker took advantage of the situation (and nobody said he didn't) but when the very helpless Deputy Minister was feeling a great weight of debt to Walker, the latter brought up the subject of land to accommodate the Agricultural Society. Said Walker, "There's a piece of land lying beside the Elbow River — about a hundred acres — that would make a first class fair grounds. Do you think you could arrange something?" The government man was in no position to argue. He made a note and said that he would see what could be done as soon as he returned to Ottawa.

Sure enough, when back at his office, Burgess wrote to Walker to express gratitude and add that the Agricultural Society could have the land beside the Elbow for two dollars and fifty cents an acre. The Society didn't have much money but it didn't need much for that purchase. Walker directed the transaction of the ninety-four acres that became Calgary's Exhibition and Stampede Grounds or Victoria Park. The total cost was 235 dollars. Undoubtedly the momentary ill temper of that anonymous horse was as important to the transaction as Walker's western hospitality. And if that combination of circumstances didn't result in the *best* real estate deal in Calgary's history, it certainly became one of the most famous.

Scattered among this group of prominent citizens, posing in 1919 with the Prince of Wales at his famous EP Ranch, are Calgary's "Big Four" — the financiers of the first Calgary Stampede. Archie McLean and A.E. Cross are at the left. George Lane and Pat Burns stand with Prince Edward. Second from the right is Colonel James Walker, another dedicated Calgary booster. Had it not been for the ill temper of an anonymous horse and for Walker's rescue of the stranded Deputy Minister, Calgary may not have been so fortunate in obtaining the ninety-four acres that have always been home to the Calgary Exhibition and Stampede.

Eastern Westerners

by Tom Moore

Calgary's Chinese population can in many ways claim to be even more "western" than many citizens of other racial origins. They rank among the real pioneers of the foothills country, and have contributed much to the growth of the city.

They may not have made it to the city in the 1870s when the Mounties first established their post at the junction of the Bow and Elbow Rivers, but they were here soon afterwards. In the 1880s, when the railroad reached the city, it was their diligent labour that helped push the Canadian Pacific Railway through the Rockies, and, when the bands of steel were completed across Canada, it was natural that they should settle in the communities they had helped to open to settlement.

The first laundry in Calgary was opened by a Chinese. Some of the first restaurants were established by Orientals who, despite the great difference in their own eating habits and those of Occidentals, quickly mastered the art of preparing Western-style food. And it was a Chinese citizen, Jimmy Smith, to whom credit must go for making one of the first really substantial contributions towards the establishment of a hospital in Calgary.

It was back in the 1880s that Mrs. Cyprian Pinkham, wife of the man who was to become Anglican Bishop of Calgary, was trying to organize a hospital after she arrived from Winnipeg. The going was tough, but her campaign received a big boost when she was given six hundred dollars from Mr. Smith's estate. Jimmy Smith had died of tuberculosis in a room in the Royal Hotel because there had been no hospital accommodation available. His bequest was made in the hope that others would be more fortunate than himself.

In the early days, Chinese who had worked on the railroad founds jobs as houseboys in the homes of leading citizens, as kitchen help in hotels and at any other job that demanded

Lawyer J.C. Brokovski, like many prominent Calgarians during the prosperous early years of the new century, hired a Chinese cook. Wing Lee, pictured here in 1915, eventually returned to China and brought his son, Yee Wing, shown at right, back to Calgary.

The Hing Wah family prospered as market gardeners in small-town Calgary.

long hours and hard work. And, when they used their savings to go into business for themselves, as restaurant men, laundrymen, market gardeners and vegetable peddlers, their records of faithfulness and trustworthiness drew plenty of support and backing from former employers.

Chinese wore queues in the early days, but the style vanished when Ho Lem, father of Calgary's former alderman, George Ho Lem, led the way towards Western hair style. One of the first converts to Christianity among Calgary's Chinese citizens, Mr. Ho was baptized at Knox Presbyterian Church in 1903, and paralleled a career as a businessman with one of active church work that saw him help bring a little Chinese United Church into being.

To oldtime Calgarians, there were two institutions in the city that were exclusively Chinese. One was the annual frenzy of firecrackers that took hold in Chinatown, on Centre Street at the Bow River, on the Chinese New Year. The other was the Chinese vegetable peddler who, in fair weather and foul, brought his wares to the homes of housewives.

Driving a rickety delivery cart, pulled generally by an ancient steed that had seen better days, the Chinese peddlers were famous for the freshness of their wares, for their faithfulness to a schedule that brought them to the door at practically the same minute every week, and for the cheerfulness with which they annually bestowed Chinese lily bulbs and packages of ginger on their customers at Christmas. He vanished with the coming of the automobile, but the Chinese peddler is an institution still fondly remembered by oldtime Calgarians.

Today, third and fourth generations of native sons can be found in the Chinese community of Calgary. Handsome buildings house the Chinese Masonic Lodge and the Chinese Nationalist League. There never were any opium dens and the Chinese lottery is long gone — but Chinese are just as much a part of the Calgary scene as are cowboys and Indians, and it is no affectation when George Ho Lem wears a wide-brimmed Western hat. He belongs in it, just as much as an Indian chief belongs in his ceremonial headdress.

In 1901 a Chinese-Presbyterian mission was formed where volunteer teachers taught English to newly settled Chinese immigrants. Although eventually the mission became non-denominational, Reverend James Chalmers Herman of Knox Presbyterian Church (at centre of photo) maintained an active interest, and converts to his faith helped to establish a little Chinese United Church.

Near Calgary (1886)

by Ellen Maria Standish

Ellen Maria (Greer) Standish arrived in Calgary on March 13, 1886. She was a twenty-nine-year-old mother with four little boys all of whom were less than nine years of age.

It is difficult to imagine, from the perspective of a hundred years, the aching loneliness of the bleak prairies. Young women like Ellen Standish, often from privileged, socially conscious eastern families, were transplanted to tiny communities of the North-West Territories barely beyond the roughest frontier stage of development. That many survived the shock is a wonder; that some thrived with good-humoured adaptability is cause for their descendants to applaud their courage.

Oh Mother! I am settled now in my new prairie home,

And the scenery that surrounds me is grand to look upon.

To my right, the glittering Rockies, of their beauty you have heard,

But yet their grandeur, Mother, by no pen can be transferred.

To my left, the great Bow River, with its ever rippling song,

Where the buffalo often quenched his thirst, beneath the midday sun.

To tell you all the sights I see would fill up all this sheet,

Of the thousand head of cattle here, that thank no man for what they eat.

Our home, it's no great mansion, just a neat little rancher's cot

Three rooms, a kitchen and parlor, which many a one has not.

The neighbours, they are far apart and do not often meet,

But one needs no invitation, for there's always lots to eat.

Remember me to all my friends, who miss my clattering tongue,

And say there're homesteads waiting here for those who care to come.

Starting a new home in tiny frontier towns too often meant isolation and longing for families left back East, but this Calgary homemaker of 1900 stands proudly on her new doorstep.

35

Deerfoot was a wild, hard-drinking man who disliked and distrusted white people. But he loved to run.

Deerfoot

by Hugh Dempsey

Hugh A. Dempsey, CM, LLD, is Assistant Director (Collections) and Chief Curator of the Glenbow Museum, Calgary.

Dr. Dempsey first became interested in history as a result of his involvement with Indians. As a newspaper reporter in 1949, he was sent to cover a meeting of the Indian Association of Alberta and while there became interested in the problems of the contemporary Indian. He began a study of general history so that Native history could be placed in its proper perspective, and began a life-long career.

As author/editor of eleven books including Red Crow: Warrior Chief, Charcoal's World and Crowfoot, Chief of the Blackfeet, Dr. Dempsey has explained the ancient culture of Native people and introduced many Canadians to the fascination of their history.

The Deerfoot Trail, which cuts a wide swath through the heart of East Calgary, was named for a Blackfoot Indian who was famous as a long distance runner, but notorious for his role as the object of a great Canadian manhunt.

When discovered by "Lying" Allen and his coterie of Calgary gamblers in 1884, Deerfoot was known as Scabby Dried Meat, and was a nephew of the great Chief Crowfoot. He was described as "one or two inches over six feet in his deerskin moccasins, and he weighed perhaps 165 pounds". He was a wild, arrogant, hard-drinking man who disliked and distrusted white people. But he loved to run.

In the 1880s, foot racing, or pedestrianism, was one of the most crooked sports around, and in Calgary it was in the hands of men who commonly fixed horse and foot races. In fact, the *Calgary Herald* complained about the problem, saying that "put up jobs are the order of the day in every class of competition" and that there was "palpable trickery in almost every class or event to which the attention of the sporting public here is directed."

Scabby Dried Meat had a few minor races in 1884, but it was not until 1886 that Calgary had the facilities for indoor events. In that year the Star Rink was built, and the first event was a "go as you please" race: four hours a night for four nights, the winner being the person who covered the most laps. The contenders were Constable James Green of the North-West Mounted Police, a former professional runner from Montreal; Little Plume, a Blackfoot who had run professionally in Winnipeg; and Scabby Dried Meat. By the third night, when the latter was well in the lead, some gamblers, who had their money on Green, got the leader drunk, but he showed up the next morning and had an easy victory. At this point his backers concluded that the name Scabby Dried Meat was not romantic enough, so they re-named him Deerfoot.

During the summer of 1886, the Indian had a few more races and in the fall the gamblers organized another big event, featuring J.W. Stokes of Birmingham, England; George Irvine of Winnipeg; Deerfoot; and a Peigan Indian named Bad Dried Meat (confusingly similar in name to Scabby Dried Meat but not the same person). It was such an important race that it was even being covered for the *New York Sporting World*. Deerfoot led the race from the first, but, when it was over, Stokes' handlers claimed there had been a miscount and their man had won by a full lap. The crowds were astounded and Deerfoot was furious when the judges, all gamblers, sustained the claim. Friends of Deerfoot raised a purse of twenty-five dollars for the loser, but the Indian refused to take it, and the *Calgary Tribune* commented that the race was "an instance of the most consummate meanness, and the men who would lend themselves to the perpetration of such a fraud deserve to be made an example of."

As a result of the scandal, the owners of the Star Rink scheduled another race, this one for ten miles, the winner to receive the medal offered at the previous race but now held by the rink. Deerfoot said he would run, but when he arrived at the rink he was suspicious and hostile. First, he found that he would be paid only on the basis of gate receipts, and Calgarians, disgusted by the last race, had not appeared. When he learned he would get only fifteen dollars and fifty cents for running, he refused to participate. Then, when the purse was raised to twenty-five dollars, he agreed to run, but wanted the track checked to see that no one had spread broken glass on it to cut his moccasined feet.

When the race finally got under way, Deerfoot at first declined to start, but finally joined when Stokes had already covered six laps. Deerfoot passed him five laps later and completed the ten miles in fifty-four minutes and thirty seconds. Stokes' handlers tried to claim that Deerfoot had disqualified himself by entering the race late, but the Indian at last received his medal and money.

Deerfoot was so disgusted that he refused to race again until the summer of 1887. As he was returning to his reserve with a bunch of friends, they robbed a settler's house. And, since there had been a rash of incidents between the Blackfoot and settlers during the year, including the killing of an Indian and the wounding of a white man near High River, many people were nervous about Indians.

When the theft was discovered the police tried to arrest Deerfoot, but he held them off with an axe and dashed away to his reserve. There he was hidden by his friends.

The Blackfoot, already upset about the killing at High River, were not inclined to co-operate with the police. Soon headlines in newspapers all across Canada were predicting that an Indian war was ready to break out. The Honourable Edgar Dewdney, Lieutenant-Governor of the North-West Territories, travelled to the Blackfoot Reserve to convince Crowfoot that his nephew should be surrendered, and, when this didn't work, a raiding party of more than a hundred Mounted Police from Calgary and Fort Macleod swept the reserve in a fruitless hunt for the fugitive.

Deerfoot was never caught. The only major incident that occurred during the manhunt happened in 1888 when a police scout shot and wounded a man he thought was Deerfoot. It turned out to be the Peigan runner Bad Dried Meat, and the government had to pay him compensation.

Finally, in the spring of 1889, Crowfoot made arrangements for Deerfoot to surrender. His case was handled by Sir James A. Lougheed and he was given only thirty days in the guardhouse.

After he served his term he was a hero among the Indians but his livelihood was gone. While he had been a fugitive, foot racing had been replaced by bicycle racing and the gamblers had left town. Deerfoot started a rapid decline and soon was rejected by Calgarians for being a ferocious troublemaker who was constantly being thrown in jail for fighting, mistreating his family, petty theft, and gambling. He pulled a knife on a man who caught him ransacking a house and was finally sent to Regina jail for beating up a fellow Indian. There, in a dank cell, he is believed to have contracted tuberculosis and, when he was arrested again in February 1897, he was a sick and broken man who died shortly afterwards in the Calgary guardhouse. According to Indian tradition, local citizens did not want him to be buried in a white cemetery so he was interred on the grounds of the Mounted Police barracks. It was Calgary's ultimate rejection of one of the town's greatest sports figures of the nineteenth century.

When the race got under way, Deerfoot at first declined to start, but finally joined after the leader had already covered six laps. Deerfoot caught and passed him to win the ten mile contest in fifty-four minutes and thirty seconds, making his mark as one of Calgary's greatest sports figures.

How the Sarcees Came to Calgary

by Hugh Dempsey

Had it not been for the determination of warrior chief Bull Head, the Sarcee Indians would now be living fifty miles east of Calgary, instead of on its western outskirts.

The two year struggle which put the Sarcees where they are today occurred more than a century ago, with Bull Head on one side and the Canadian government on the other.

The story goes back to 1877, when the tribes of southern Alberta signed Treaty Seven, and the government expected the Sarcees, Blackfoot and Bloods to live together as one happy family near Blackfoot Crossing. However, although the Sarcees were allied to the Blackfoot, they were never close friends.

During the winter of 1878-79, the Sarcees were induced to move to their reserve, but when they reached Fort Calgary they refused to go any further. They claimed there had been an argument with the Blackfoot over the distribution of flour and they did not wish to camp with them. By July, 1879 they were finally persuaded to go to the Crossing, but on the opposite side of the river from the Blackfoot. The peaceful valley soon echoed with the sounds of quarrels, interspersed with the noise of rifle shots across the quiet Bow River.

After the treaty payments, the Sarcees left Blackfoot Crossing and Bull Head vowed his people would never settle there. They moved to Fort Calgary for the winter of 1879-80, while the Blackfoot followed the buffalo into Montana. With the country depleted of game, the Sarcees were given rations by the Mounted Police, but only if they returned to their reserve. The situation was intolerable. There was constant bickering with the Blackfoot and there was always some kind of trouble. So when a mixup occurred and the ration supply gave out, the tribe found a reason to go back to their favourite camping grounds at Calgary, where they demanded food. Fearful for their safety, the three-man Mounted Police detachment sent a courier to Fort Macleod for help. Immediately, a detachment of thirty men accompanied by the Indian agent came north, and a council was held.

When it was obvious that they would not move to their reserve, the agent suggested they go to Fort Macleod, where there were sufficient police to issue rations and keep them in line. Bull Head preferred Calgary but was told if he stayed, his people would receive no food. The chief reluctantly agreed, and in spite of mid-winter conditions the destitute tribe set out. After several days on the trail, they ran into a blizzard in the vicinity of the present town of Stavely. It was bitterly cold and impossible to travel, so the Indians camped in a coulee for three days until the storm had eased. By then the rations were almost gone, so the Mounted Police escort set out alone for Fort Macleod to get help. Provisions were then sent to meet the Indians and they were escorted to Fort Macleod for the rest of the winter.

By the spring of 1881, Ottawa had grown weary of the "on again off again" Sarcee Reserve, and demanded that the issue be settled. "Their dislike of the Blackfoot Crossing," the Indian agent reported, "was having their reserve in common with the Blackfoot. This we overcame by showing them that they would be entirely independent of the Blackfoot, who would be asked to give up

40

Bull Head

41

any right they might have to this land. The Bow River would form a decided boundary between them and they would have an instructor of their own."

Bull Head then aired his own views as to the location of a reserve for the Sarcees. He told the agent they wanted a place "on Fish Creek, eight miles above the supply farm," on the western outskirts of Calgary.

Although not happy with the government's decision, Bull Head reluctantly agreed to take his tribe back to Blackfoot Crossing, provided that land would be broken and ready for seeding when they arrived. This the agent promised.

As the Indians marched northward to their reserve and the newly broken farms, it looked as though the government had finally won its two-year battle with the tribe. But while the

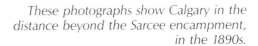

These photographs show Calgary in the distance beyond the Sarcee encampment, in the 1890s.

Indians were on the trail, the Indian agent received an anxious message from Blackfoot Crossing which wiped out all his careful manoeuvring. It stated that the contractor "has not ploughed any land for the Sarcees," and that "the Sarcees, if they can only find a little excuse, are liable to turn back, if everything that was promised them is not fulfilled."

But here Bull Head proved that he was a wise politician who could turn defeat into victory. Instead of resorting to force, the chief had a man write a letter to Ottawa, outlining the details of the unfulfilled agreement.

Three months later, he held a council with Indian commissioner Edgar Dewdney and got what he wanted: a reserve on Fish Creek, on the western outskirts of Calgary. On the final play in a two year game of nerves, Bull Head held the winning hand.

Dr. Robert David Sanson

by Gina Newton

Gina A. Newton is the daughter of Mr. and Mrs. D.C. Newton, granddaughter of Mr. and Mrs. A.C. Newton, and great-granddaughter of Dr. and Mrs. R.D. Sanson, all of whom have made their home in Calgary. Gina is at present a student at Western Canada High School in Calgary.

Dr. Robert David Sanson, my great-grandfather, was a native of Toronto and came to Calgary in 1892 following his graduation from Upper Canada College, Trinity University and the University of Edinburgh.

On his arrival in Calgary, he became affiliated with the North-West Mounted Police as Medical Officer. In 1893 he went to Toronto to marry Miss Beatrice Webber and returned with his bride to Calgary to establish his home and a medical practice. Dr. and Mrs. Sanson lived in a white, two story house on Fourth Avenue, behind the Cathedral Church of the Redeemer. The ground floor of the house was used as an office, with an adjoining waiting room in which a parrot talked to the patients.

As a general practitioner, he was well liked by friends and patients alike. He was a very musical man and played the piano by ear, so he was often asked to play the organ in the Cathedral. Friends who knew him have described him as tall and handsome with a dignified, impressive presence.

One of my great-grandfather's patients was an Indian who had appendicitis. When their medicine man could not heal him, the tribe brought him to the General Hospital by wagon. The operation was successful, fortunately, because the Indian's relatives had set up their tee-pees outside of the hospital and who knows what could have happened if the outcome had been different! Another incident did not end as happily. A patient went berserk and stabbed my great-grandfather in the hand with a scalpel. He lost the use of three fingers, and he was never to operate again, although somehow he managed to continue playing the piano.

During the First World War, he was attached to the Eighth Field Ambulance Corps, and, later on, continuing his military affiliation, Dr. Sanson became the director of the Colonel Belcher Hospital.

After his wife's death he lived at Braemar Lodge, Calgary's well-known residential hotel,

Nurses, taking a late afternoon break from their duties at the General Hospital, visit the Indians camped nearby.

and was frequently seen on summer Sundays wearing white flannels, jacket and tie, playing golf at the Calgary Golf and Country Club.

Thanks to his daughter, Marian Newton, my grandmother, I have attained this information about a wonderful doctor and man, Dr. R.D. Sanson.

Dr. Robert David Sanson was tall and handsome with a dignified impressive presence.

The Van Wart Family Chronicles

by Hallé Palfrey

Hallé (Van Wart) Palfrey was born in Calgary, the daughter of wealthy pioneer businessman Isaac Van Wart. She spent her childhood in the comfort of the family home which, along with the Lougheed residence across the street, was a city landmark of some distinction.

In 1914 the family returned to Ontario where Van Wart retired, but in later years Mrs. Palfrey came back to Calgary where she made a home with her own family until her death in 1983.

As soon as the railway came through and it was evident that Calgary would be a prospering community, Isaac Van Wart came west to see for himself what opportunities might lie in store for his family. He was an ambitious young man of thirty-four in 1887, with two children, and was willing to work hard, so when he realized that a lumber trade would expand right alongside the growing town, he soon learned all there was to know about the business.

Establishing himself as one of the community's founding pillars, Isaac Van Wart set up house (in the sandstone

The details of the domestic tragedy are lost now, but, for reasons of her own, the first Mrs. Van Wart left her husband to run away with a travelling circus performer. The life evidently wasn't as glamorous as might have been expected though, because soon the two children returned to their father, although their mother did not come back. Isaac, however, wasted little time grieving over lost causes, and in 1900 returned to London, Ontario and married Hattie Jaynes, the sixteen-year-old daughter of his closest friend.

Isaac returned to Calgary with Hattie, and moved into a large brick house on Eighth Avenue East — large enough at least to house the teenage children of the first marriage as well as their own baby son, who arrived the following year. By this time the lumber business had taken firm hold and Father was positioning himself in the community as one of its founding pillars, becoming President of the Board of Trade and first President of the Calgary Exhibition — a post he held from 1907 to 1913.

As the family continued to grow, Father bought the A.L. Sifton house across the street from Sir James and Lady Lougheed on Sixth Street and Thirteenth Avenue, and four of the next six children were born there. We were a privileged group of youngsters, fortunate to have all the accoutrements of the eastern well-to-do. Governesses, nurses, maids and grooms entertained and kept us out of trouble. Yet at the same time Calgary was such a small and friendly community that our mother felt quite confident about putting two of us toddlers into the pony cart for a solitary ride down to the lumber yard on Ninth Avenue and First Street West. The pony was so well trained, though, that he moved at barely a walk, and, when our destination had been reached, no amount of coaxing would budge him further. He simply turned and made the leisurely journey back home again.

The only really serious issue of contention I remember between my parents was caused when my father faced the possibility of becoming Calgary's hangman. In 1901 Father began his eight-year office as sheriff, and was faced at one point with carrying out the execution of a man who was connected with the illegal whiskey trade and convicted of murder. The official hangman had been delayed; if he didn't arrive at the appointed hour, Father would have to do the job himself. Mother was furious! She threatened to leave and take all of us with her.

structure pictured at the right) across the street from the Lougheeds.

Hattie Van Wart and groom, Ted Mayhew, prepare her beautifully matched team and carriage for an early Calgary horse show.

I presume that the executioner arrived in time, however, because we all stayed together for our move to the summer house in Banff. Father had bought the original Banff train station and had it moved up the Avenue and remodelled for our use as a vacation home. One year we were caught there by the arrival of another baby, so we spent that glorious full year in the log cabin.

Life continued back home as usual: Father as patriarch of his large clan of children and leader of the community, and Mother as social convenor of the whole group. As was the custom in those days, Mother held an "At Home" each week. On her specified afternoon, guests were welcome to call for a short visit and would be served tea and cookies — carefully prepared by our Chinese cook, Sing.

Now Sing was a temperamental sort, but left to himself he was quite happy to putter about the kitchen preparing really excellent meals. Most of us learned to keep out of his way, but our groom, Ted Mayhew, was a tease. One afternoon, Mayhew, beckoned by the smells of the freshly baked treats for Mother's "At Home", sneaked into Sing's kitchen and reached silently for a sample from the cooling rack. Instantly Sing lunged for his cleaver and whacked off Mayhew's nose!

Justice was swift, but the penalty long. Sing was tried and imprisoned, but at the end of his sentence he was unable to leave the jail. So enthusiastic were his jailers and fellow inmates about his cooking that Sing was urged to stay on. Mother's loss became the gain of pioneer Calgary's seedier element.

David Crowchild

by Hugh Dempsey

The name "Crowchild" is inextricably linked with Calgary through the busy Crowchild Trail and the other place-names within the city. The name is a tribute to a popular Sarcee patriarch whose family has done much to maintain good will and friendship between his people and Calgarians.

David Crowchild was born on the Sarcee Reserve on April 12, 1899, the son of Mark Crowchild and Sarah Big Plume. David's mother was a niece of treaty chief Bull Head.

When David was eight years old, he was enrolled in St. Barnabas Anglican Residential School on the Sarcee Reserve, and stayed there until he was eighteen. During that time he ran away only once, and even then it was just for a day. The routine was that students got only the month of July off, and were back in school on the first of August.

David had reached Form Four in school when he was discharged in 1917. He started farming on twenty to thirty acres of land, and also raised horses. He became interested in rodeos and, although he never won any trophies, he sometimes took day money in bronc riding, wild horse racing, and calf roping. He also took part in chuck wagon racing, democrat racing, and a once-popular competition called cattle yelling. For the next twenty years he was involved in rodeoing, and worked behind the chutes of the Calgary Stampede. "It was lots of fun," he said.

Shortly after he was out of school, David met a Sioux girl named Daisie Dawn, who was married to a man named Crane, a Stoney from Morley who had been transferred to the Sarcees. In May, 1929, after Crane died, David married Daisie. He inherited a family of three by her previous marriage and then had five children of his own.

David Crowchild, Chief of the Sarcees, recognized the need to preserve his culture, and, at the same time, to make his own living in a modern society. He was the "goodwill ambassador" between the Sarcees and Calgarians.

Although David had spent considerable time off the reserve attending rodeos and stampedes, his interest in the economic problems of his people began in earnest in 1945, when he attended a meeting of the Indian Association of Alberta. There he established a lifelong friendship with John Laurie, a Calgary schoolteacher who was helping to organize the Indians.

"The first time I met him," recalled Mr. Crowchild, "I called him Mr. Laurie, but he said to call him John, like the others did. He looked just like a farmer and seemed to have a real bitterness about the way that white people were treating the Indians." The two became so inseparable that David adopted Laurie as his brother.

Crowchild often appeared in Native costume at meetings and official functions to proudly illustrate the ancient culture that was his heritage.

In 1946, when the Sarcee leader Joe Big Plume died, everybody wondered who would be the next chief. A nominating meeting was called and although David did not attend, his name was among the twenty put forward. When the election was held, David Crowchild obtained the largest number of votes and became the tribal chief, while the two runners up were named as councillors.

During his seven-year term as chief, David brought in a system of regular reporting and of making minutes available. His term also saw the construction of a modern school on the reserve, the establishment of the first large band farm in southern Alberta, development of the band cattle herd, improvement of roads, and the availability of an education in Calgary for Sarcee students who wanted it.

But probably David's most important role was as a link between Calgary and the Sarcee Reserve. Before his death on April 9, 1982, he and his wife had established a longtime record as constant good will ambassadors, appearing either in Native costume or everyday clothes to participate in meetings and official functions. They spoke frequently in schools and to young people, their friendliness and gentleness creating a good image of the Sarcee people.

David was a part of today's world, yet he retained much of the pride and spirit of his ancestors. He recognized the need to preserve his culture and, at the same time, to make his own living in modern society. This he had done successfully throughout his life as a farmer and rancher.

50

G.D. Stanley, Pioneer Doctor and Politician

by Lillian McAra and Walter Johns

Lillian (Stanley) McAra is the daughter of Dr. G.D. Stanley, a well known physician, politician and historian of Calgary's past. Mrs. McAra has been active in volunteer work all of her adult life, serving with the Samaritan Club, the Junior Service League and the Canadian Red Cross, and as a director on the board of the Alberta Rehabilitation Council for the Disabled.

Walter Johns, MD, received his medical education from the University of Alberta and practised medicine and anaesthesiology at the Calgary Associate Clinic from 1942 to 1957. He was head of the Department of Anaesthesiology at the Holy Cross Hospital, the General Hospital and the Children's Hospital, and has served as president of the Calgary Medical Society and on numerous committees of The College of Physicians and Surgeons. Dr. Johns' recollections of his old friend G.D. Stanley are included here.

My father, it was said, was harder to contain than a prairie blizzard in a hat box! Such was his enthusiasm for life that he met the challenges of medical and political careers with energy and humour and lived, despite the dire predictions of his youth, to be a vigorous old man.

When he graduated from the University of Toronto Medical School in 1901, a lingering chest infection, probably tuberculosis, made him too ill to set up practice in the East, and he decided to risk a trip west to look for the sunshine, clean air and rugged life that might improve his chances.

When his train arrived in High River, Dad stepped on to the platform to see how close he might be getting to the prescribed atmosphere. A western gentleman, no doubt spying Dad's brand-new black medical bag, approached and begged for relief from an agonizing toothache. Of course Dad was no dentist, but the cowboy pleaded with him and finally convinced him that the emergency warranted immediate treatment.

A pair of pliers was found, the afflicted tooth was displayed, and Dad yanked. The offending tooth flew out all right, but the pliers slipped, hit another decayed tooth on the other side of the mouth and knocked that one out too! His reputation was made. Patients flocked in, and as Dad said many years later, "I got over the idea of dying long ago."

His was a country practice of far-flung patients, involving long cold journeys to house calls accompanied by a team of black horses that pulled his buggy and sleigh. In 1910, however, he was one of the first in Alberta to experiment with the automobile. Evidently the provincial secretary knew of Dad's hit-or-miss experiences with the new car because when he issued him a license plate, the sixth in the province, he declared that Dad must be lucky in numbers. "When you get caught for speeding," he said, "all you'll have to do is turn the plate upside down and start over with a new number."

That much-scarred automobile accompanied Dad to political meetings between 1913 and 1921 when he was a Member of the Alberta Legislature. The taste of politics in High River whetted his appetite for the bigger arena of Calgary, so after he moved to the big city he served as Conservative Member of Parliament in Calgary East and accompanied R.B. Bennett to Ottawa for the new Prime Minister's tenure from 1930 to 1935.

The Depression era was not a happy time for Conservative politicians, and Dad groaned as the Liberals made steady inroads with every election. One day when Parliament was in session, Dad noticed that a valuable political ally was missing and, upon inquiring about his absence, was told that he was on his honeymoon. Gossip had it that "Joe" had married a particularly charming young blonde half his age. "Damn!" said Dad, "There goes another by-election!"

Facing Page: *G.D. Stanley, frontier doctor, was harder to contain than a prairie blizzard in a hat box!*

Just a Recollection

Anonymous

Calgary was a nice little town in 1906 even with its wooden sidewalks and muddy streets. We were a delightful mix of people: most had come here from the British Isles, many came from the States, and a few German and Russian folks lived over in Riverside. The Chinese, who worked in laundries or restaurants, or on the CPR tracks, wore their hair in long pigtails. They sent their pay back to China to support their families because their wives weren't allowed to come to Canada in those days.

My family lived at Second Street and Third Avenue West — right at the centre of all the commerce of the city, and just as close to the Eau Claire Mill that was our playground year round. In winter, when the driver delivered our fire wood, he was good-humoured enough to let us tie our sleds behind his wagon so that his plodding horse could pull us along on a free ride. And, in the summer, all the neighbourhood kids spent hours rafting on the water that spilled over the mill dam. We stood spellbound on the little bridge between the mill and Prince's Island

Calgary was just about perfect in those days, even with its wooden sidewalks and muddy streets, because we children could wander freely all over town. I remember the penny candy stores, the wagon hauling firewood and the Indians camped at the edge of town who sold lovely willow baskets and bark ornaments.

watching as the Bow River, bringing the logs down from the forests of the foothills, rushed over the spillway. Lumber was piled on Prince's Island, and there was always a cool spot under each stack where we used to crawl to pick wild strawberries which grew in abundance.

Our winters really *were* colder, but as soon as a chinook arrived, the women got busy at the pumps. Wash boilers were filled with water heated on coal stoves, scrub boards and tubs made ready and soon the clotheslines were filled with family laundry. Anxiously, everyone watched the western sky for signs that the weather was about to change. Then flat-irons finished the drying process so that the clean clothes could be folded away before the cold settled in once again. When that happened, we all returned once again to our customary wintertime hardships. The milkman always had trouble finishing his route before the milk froze too hard to be poured from the big cans. One time, I remember, he borrowed Mother's big heavy butcher knife to hack off the high tower from the top of the can, only to break the knife against the frozen cream!

Children in those days wandered freely all over town. It's hard to imagine now, but the block on which Eaton's now stands was open prairie where the Indians pitched their tents when they came to town to sell their handmade willow baskets and bark ornaments at the homes of well-to-do Calgarians. There were lovely homes then; from Second to Seventh Avenues big houses with spacious grounds and terraced gardens housed the leading citizens of the day. One very cold Christmas Dr. Lafferty cut down a huge spruce tree from his front lawn because the Indians, who usually brought in a tree for the First Baptist Church Christmas concert, couldn't make the trip through the heavy snows, and "What would a carol concert be without a Christmas tree?"

Dr. Lafferty's gift to our Christmas concert was the spruce tree he chopped down from the front yard of his lovely home, "Rubble Hill".

Our first school was an old red brick building, but the floors were so thin we were soon moved to the new Central School. Many had to come quite a distance on horseback, all the way from Shouldice, carrying lunches in Burns' Shamrock lard pails. We all thought it wonderful if some windfall brought us a nickel to spend after school. Fred Langston, who ran our neighbourhood grocery store, had all the patience in the world while we chose our penny candy, but as soon as the trade was completed we were shuffled out the door, with just enough grace to keep us coming back. You see, he had to compete for our business against Charlie Bloomfield's gorgeous home-made candies, and Rochon's Eastertime specials. Come to think of it — Calgary was just about perfect in those days of my childhood!

The Visionary

by Margaret Hare

Margaret Hare was told the story of the Harrigan family by her brother-in-law, Vincent Harrigan — a baby born in a stable on a summer's day in 1906.

Miss Hare was born in Scotland but came to Canada in 1911 and settled with her family in the East. When her sister married Vince Harrigan and urged her mother to join the young family in Calgary, Margaret and her mother packed their belongings and moved west.

Mr. and Mrs. D.P. Harrigan, moving from Ontario to Calgary in 1906, found the train journey a long and tiresome one. However, leaving the downtown station behind them, their spirits soared as they noted the high blue skies and the fresh clean air. Almost immediately it became love at first sight, and grew stronger with the passing years.

Housekeeping accommodation was difficult to find at the time. However, Mr. Harrigan procured a small piece of land at the corner of Fifteenth Avenue and Eighth Street Southwest and built a low rectangular shack consisting of a kitchen-sitting-room, a bedroom and a stable, which housed a horse, a cow, and some chickens. It was in this little shack, next door to the animals, that a baby boy was born the following August. The Oblate Fathers baptized him Vincent David Leo Harrigan.

The family later moved to Eighteenth Avenue and Second Street West across from the Indians' hitching post. Two years later an epidemic of typhoid fever broke out in Calgary and district, and little Vincent became ill with the contagious disease. He was told that he was one of the first patients in the D'Youville ward of the Holy Cross Hospital.

A short time later his father bought some land north of Calgary in the area now known as Thorncliffe. Mr. Harrigan farmed there for several years, but moved down to the Mission district about 1912, where the family lived for many years. During this period Vincent remembered the Blackfoot and Sarcee Indians having a pow-wow once a week at the corner of Nineteenth Avenue and Second Street West. One can imagine the little boy gazing awe-struck at all the pomp and ceremony, wishing no doubt that he was one of the tribe, and wondering why his parents didn't join the lively group.

In 1909, his grandfather joined the family in Calgary and became very good friends with

Grandfather made friends with Father Doucet, who for many years ministered to the Indians living near Calgary. Here in this 1919 photo, Chief Big Belly poses beside the Catholic mission church at the Sarcee Reserve.

little Vince. They often went together to visit the Lacombe Home, and thus became acquainted with Father Lacombe and Father Doucet, who was the first white man to meet Colonel Macleod at the junction of the Bow and Elbow Rivers in 1875. Father Doucet was then living in a tent with the Indians, and evidently made such an impression on Vincent's grandfather that the old man donated the altar in his honour to the Lacombe Home in 1911.

In 1912 the little boy and his grandfather attended the first organized Stampede. The grandstand was then situated at the north side of the old race track. They put on a great show, even in those early days.

Vincent started school that same year at St. Mary's School on Nineteenth Avenue and Second Street West. His first teacher was Esther Gardner, a sister of Herb Gardner, the famous defence player for the Montreal Canadiens. In his second year at primary school he met Pat Burns' son, Michael. Michael was a lonely little boy living with his father and a housekeeper, and many times Vincent was invited to have dinner with the Burns family. After the meal, the little boys used to work hard trying to make little red wagons, sleighs or bird-houses.

The next step was high school in the old Oblate building on Seventeenth Avenue South. There were about sixty boys attending when Vincent did, and many brought honours to their school. Vincent's days of glory, however, involved the Blue Dandies, the band that he and a few other boys formed. Alphonse Gerard played drums, Bill Allen the saxophone, Leo McKinnon the violin, and George Prieur the banjo; Vincent played the piano. They were happy days with practices at one another's homes and performances at parties and dances at the old Cochrane Hall. The band lasted about two years, but was brought to a halt when the boys split up to go to university.

Vincent was the first student to register at St. Joseph's College on campus at the University of Alberta in Edmonton. He graduated in pharmacy in 1929 and was ready to go to face the world. For several years he practised at Dunford Drugs, and then worked as a travelling sales representative for a major drug company.

Vince often commented about the dreams and aspirations of the old pioneers, but of course they didn't live to see many of their dreams fulfilled. I was prompted on hearing his story to write this poem.

The Visionary

Don't pity the old pioneer,
Who wrestled and strove with the plough.
He wouldn't change places with you,
Who are reaping the benefits now.

He died in the morn of his dreams,
With the dawn breaking over the rim,
Wrapped in the vision he saw,
And the future still calling to him.

Don't pity that long ago man.
His way was the better by far,
Dreaming his dreams as he trudged along,
With his old plough hitched to a star.

It was in a rough little shack, undoubtedly similar to this one, with animals sheltered nearby, that baby Vince Harrigan was born.

Early Calgary was the hub of horse and cattle country. Here, in the fabled wide-open spaces, many, like Arthur Rawlinson pictured here, acquired nimble mounts and flung themselves into competitive polo matches.

Arthur Barrett, Where Are You?

by Jack Peach

Jack Peach is a native Calgarian whose lifelong interest in people and their stories has made him an historical raconteur of the highest calibre. He sold his first piece of writing at the age of nine and began broadcasting three years later. His career with the CBC opened the way for his broadcast reminiscences which in turn created a demand for his collections of local historical adventures called Peach Preserves *and* Peach Cordial. *"Arthur Barrett, Where Are You" is a delicious taste of a perfect Peach creation.*

In the late 1800s Calgary was the hub of horse and cattle country. Newcomers were pouring into the empty land, many of them from England, bringing with them their customs, habits and enthusiasms, not the least of which was the game of polo. Here in the fabled wide-open spaces many acquired nimble mounts and flung themselves into competitive polo matches. The high calibre of the contests soon made the names of Calgary, High River, Pekisko, Millarville and Macleod well known in international polo circles.

In Calgary the matches were played in what today is Elbow Park, close by the Glencoe Club. There were two race tracks on the flat prairie land alongside the Elbow River; one track was within the other, thus providing race ovals of two lengths. In the centre of the tracks was the polo field. In time, the land was sold for building lots and Elbow Park developer Fred Lowes had his company surveyors stake out a large tract that encompassed the race tracks and the polo field. Nobody seemed to know who the culprit was but one night every survey stake was pulled out and spirited away, and a polo match took place as scheduled the following day.

In 1907 Calgary's polo team had been on a long winning streak and managed to arrange a challenge match with the finest California team at Del Coronado Beach on the United States' west coast. There was great excitement, anticipation and celebration, with all the horses and all but one player, whose name was Arthur Barrett, receiving a rousing send-off at the railway station on the start of their journey to a truly international polo match.

Barrett was a very independent fellow who had persuaded his team mates to let him make the journey on his own. Since he was one of the most experienced players and had been a member of the British Army team in India, it was decided to humour the chap. Everyone was in a benign and jovial mood, having been wined and dined lavishly in anticipation of their international success, and they agreed to Arthur's request.

About a month after the California game was played and won, without the help of Barrett, the team received a cable from England asking, "Where are you fellows and the horses?" Arthur Barrett, not a little befuddled by the anticipatory celebrations, had gone the wrong way!

Arthur Barrett, appearing here at the centre of these mounted riders, played polo for the Millarville team in 1907.

Poor Butterfly

by Ruth Gorman

Dr. Ruth Gorman, the daughter of early Calgary lawyer M.B. Peacock, was raised to expect that she would contribute actively to the social well-being of her community. She graduated from the faculty of law at the University of Alberta but, because of the traditional 1940s expectations of young matrons, it was assumed that she would not work as a lawyer. She would stay home to raise her baby, keep house and become yet another upper middle class club woman. Instead she combined roles, volunteered her services to the Local Council of Women and spent a lifetime as counsel to those without a legal voice. She represented countless consumer groups, led a five year battle for the Indian rights movement and circulated the proud stories of our western heritage through her magazine, Golden West.

In the pre-First World War era, when women trailed long deforming skirts in the dust and didn't have the vote, they agitated for change, not like wasps, but more like honey bees.

At that time the women's clubs — like the Country Women's Institute and The Local Council of Women — held their meetings in the women's own domain, the private homes of the membership. There they discussed problems, not pompously from a podium, but quietly over fragile tea cups. Most of the women were married, some were wealthy, but all were concerned about the tragedy of their less fortunate sisters — the neglected victims of male exploiters who left these women pregnant without any financial resources to aid in raising the illegitimate children. The club women knew, in those pre-pill days, that biology played no favourites. The victims were as often naive young girls as ladies-of-the-night — "Poor Butterflies", to use the ladylike vernacular of the day. As the ladies said, "The men can have their fun and just walk away!" This was not an age of state care; there were only orphanages run by the church or dedicated individuals such as Reverend George Wood. The situation was tragic and the club women looked frantically for a solution.

Leadership for the cause fell naturally to Nellie McClung. She was a remote relative of mine so I have a fine memory of her. She was a big women with a face that was usually clear and calm and radiated warmth, and a tongue that was always witty. An author, whose books reflect the cheerfulness and faith of her outlook, she had not only adopted a parentless child herself, but had written a best seller about the venture called *Sowing Seeds In Danny*.

Mrs. McClung had lots of help because pioneer Calgary had many able women who were concerned for their community. What they lacked in university-trained talent they made up in native wit and determination. Over their tea cups these virtuous women decided that something should be done to assist the mothers of illegitimate children. Their discussions were slightly hampered because all sex words were strictly taboo, but despite that they made their meaning clear with a raised eyebrow here or a weary sigh there. It was decided after gentle debate that Nellie should be sent to Edmonton to discuss the matter with Premier Charles Stewart. He was known as a church-goer, so it was hoped he would be sympathetic to their cause.

Nellie returned to Calgary in triumph. The Premier had assured her he would introduce legislation by which any mother of an illegitimate child could, if she could give proof of parentage, legally demand from the father some financial support for her child's birth, food and clothing. The ladies got busy and subtly hustled supporting votes from other members of the Legislature and the Act was passed.

The next problem was to get a positive test case in court. How to find a Poor Butterfly, complete with babe in arms, to prove the new legislation? Finally such a girl was located and she was persuaded to go to court to face that all-male body, name her seducer and demand financial assistance to raise the child.

On the day in question the good ladies decided to attend the trial. Most carefully wore veils on their hats, but in happy anticipation they filled the back rows of the court. To their obvious delight Butterfly appeared, and, upon prodding from her lawyer, finally admitted to having had intercourse with John Doe. John Doe, under oath, admitted his guilt and the ladies murmured with obvious pleasure. But their delight was short-lived. Doe's lawyer called forth three other witnesses, all rather seedy, slightly soggy males who, under oath, quickly declared that they too had had intercourse with Poor Butterfly just about nine months previous to the all-important date. After careful deliberation the judge solemnly announced that since it was not clear who the actual father was, it would be unjust to make John Doe pay!

Poor Butterfly, faced with court costs and an even further besmirched name, clutched her illegitimate child, gave the crestfallen ladies one final dirty look and faded into Calgary's East End.

At the next meeting the good ladies' tea cups really rattled. Grimly it was decided that Nellie should make a second trip to Edmonton to see the Premier. The whole routine would have to be repeated.

About a year later, after arduous search, a second Poor Butterfly was located. It had taken considerable time. The story of their last defeat had spread and few unfortunates wanted to get up in the box and go through all that just for a bunch of old busybodies, but finally a test case was cornered, bribed and coerced into laying a charge and appearing in court. The ladies attended this time in a silent group. No longer had they the pleased look or even the veils, but sat rigid and anxious on the back benches of the court, carefully listening.

Poor Butterfly the Second told her sad tale. Then the second John Doe's lawyer called him to the stand and he confessed to having had relations with the woman. As in the case before, he was followed by several male friends or witnesses, and they too slyly testified as to their sexual successes with the lady in question near or on the pertinent date. The ladies nervously awaited a decision.

The verdict wasn't long in coming. "Well," said the judge, "since you men have all testified that you had intercourse with Butterfly, and any one of you could have been the father of this child, I find you will each share equally the cost of this child's birth and its upkeep until it is sixteen years of age, as is laid out in the new amendment to the Act."

The ladies' victory was a quiet one. Many a husband wondered why his wife looked so smug as she served his dinner, but it was rumoured that in the red light district, down on Seventh Avenue East, the drinks were on the house, courtesy of a certain butterfly and her allies, the honey bees.

Facing Page: *Nellie McClung's books reflected the cheerfulness and faith of her outlook; she had adopted a parentless child herself and had written a best seller about the venture. She was the logical leader for the ladies' efforts toward social change.*

Moving to Calgary in 1911

by Mary Jane Gardiner

———————————————————————————

Mary Jane Gardiner, throughout a long and sometimes difficult life, combined an iron will, a sense of purpose and a truly inexhaustible fund of good humour. Following their arrival in Calgary in 1911, Mary Jane and her husband settled into the new community and raised their family of four children from their home on Twelfth Avenue Southwest. The family attended the first Calgary Stampede which was held the next summer, and for many years Mary Jane displayed her handmade patchwork quilts at the annual exhibition.

Edward Gardiner, who possessed a fine baritone voice, sang in and directed choirs throughout the city, including the celebrated Haydn Male Quartet which toured western Canada during the 1920s.

In her mid-eighties, Mrs. Gardiner bought a typewriter and began to record her memoirs. The incident described here is an excerpt from that collection which she titled My Memories of Bygone Days.

———————————————————————————

Early in March of 1911, my husband went west to spy out the country and select a place to settle, intending to send for his wife and family. He chose Calgary, Alberta, secured a position with his old firm, and immediately sent word that we should settle up the business in Ontario and come west.

This was great news for the family. The idea of going to a new country and starting life all over was a great thrill to all of us, and I immediately got to work settling up the affairs, renting the two houses which we owned, and making ready for the long journey.

In less than three months I had leased out both homes and concluded all the business; all the furniture and effects had been crated, and were ready to be taken to the freight car which I had chartered for the trip west.

All had gone well, but I had not reckoned on meeting the world alone, and I soon found out there were plenty of dishonest people looking for an opportunity to cheat a woman. I had rented my home to two people whom I thought were a gentleman and lady, but was sadly disappointed and found out later that they were a pair of scoundrels.

My three children were all under the age of twelve years so I had prepared a wonderful hamper for our four day train journey and I included some treats for my husband, among them a whole side of back bacon and pots of marmalade and jams. I also baked a large batch of cookies for the children. The new tenants wanted to move in so I sent my furniture ahead to the station ready for loading as soon as the car which I had chartered was ready. In the meantime I took the children to a friend's home across the street to stay until we were ready to leave, and left the hamper in the house with the new tenants.

Facing Page: *The Gardiner family: he possessed a fine baritone voice, she was a woman who would not be cheated.*

The next morning I went back to our old home to make some arrangements and get my hamper, and was accosted with the news that someone had broken into the house and stolen the hamper. I asked the new tenants if the thieves had taken any of their things and they said no. I thought it funny that they should take my box and nothing else, but being rather dull in the matter of thieving, I did not suspect them of lying.

I was curious to see the place where my hamper was left so I made bold to walk into the pantry, and there on the floor were some of the cookies which the lady tenant had failed to gather up in the skirmish of removing them from the box. I knew they were mine because, in making the cookies, I was anxious that they should be extra good and had put in too much shortening. As a result, it made them bake with tiny holes, so the moment I saw the cookies, I recognized them and the thief was discovered. This upset me very much but time was short. My things were already at the station and we were due to leave the next day. Nothing could be done but leave the thieves there and put the matter in the hands of an agent to collect the rent as long as they continued to pay it.

However, my troubles weren't over. As I did not need the entire freight car for my furniture, I advertised space in a car going to Calgary, Alberta. A widow applied for a small corner for her effects, which I sold her for thirty dollars. A farmer bought space for two bulls which he was shipping to Lethbridge. I sold him one end of the car for fifty dollars, and found a man who offered to look after the cattle for a free trip and he gave me an additional ten dollars for the job. Things were going along nicely, but I had not figured on dealing with rogues.

The widow and the man who was to look after the cattle had paid me in full, but the owner of the cattle had not said a word about the pay and it was getting late.

In the meantime, a neighbour who had heard that I had sold a space to this farmer asked if he had paid me. I said no. He told me to be careful because I was dealing with a shady character, and that he would cheat me if I did not watch him closely. I took the hint and at once made my way to the freight station. Sure enough, while I waited he drove up in a great hurry and seemed surprised to find me there. He ignored me and began at once to unload his cattle from the truck. I approached and asked him to settle with me as I was also in a hurry, but he refused and said there was no rush for that. I told him to settle now or the cattle would not go in the train car. Again he refused to acknowledge my request and I saw that I had to act quickly, so I hurried back to the station, told my story, and asked an officer to return with me. He said, "Have you paid this lady yet? Pay her before you do another thing, or your cattle don't go in that car."

The scoundrel saw that he was beaten so he handed me the fifty dollars and grumpily asked for a receipt. I thanked the officer and returned to my home to make my final arrangements for the journey.

I hurried back, collected the children, bid goodbye to my old friends, my old home "Runnymede" on Richmond Street, and got back to the train in time to leave that night. Quite a number of our friends had met at the station to bid us goodbye and God speed. Among them was my husband's brother Harry, who said, "Cheer up, Mary Jane. Every mile brings you nearer to Ed." By that time, though, I was pretty well worn out and too tired for much emotion of any kind, so I collapsed on the seat and knew that I would lie there until I got to Calgary.

It was then that I realized what it meant to be alone in world, and how the world tries to take advantage of a woman. Still I am reminded of the adage, "All's well that ends well", for I got safely to Calgary and fared pretty well on my gamble with the car. It cost me 135 dollars, but I sold ninety dollars space, and got all my effects to Calgary for forty-five dollars. It was also lucky that I took the cattle for, in the case of livestock, the car had to be hurried through. Everything arrived in ten days; otherwise it might have taken months, as was the case with some of my friends who came at the same time.

Annie Davidson

by Lois Cutler

Lois Cutler is a native Calgarian. She attended city schools, and it wasn't until she was married in 1942 that she left Calgary (for the first time in her life) to go to Toronto. When Mrs. Cutler returned ten years later, she joined the Parnassus Club, a literary club founded by Georgina Thomson for young women who, for financial or other reasons, had not attended university. From that introduction Mrs. Cutler expanded her horizons in literature and in 1963 joined the Calgary Women's Literary Club. In this organization it is the custom for each member to prepare a paper about a particular topic of interest for presentation to the rest of the membership. Annie Davidson, she knew, would be her most interesting subject.

In the Memorial Library at Central Park there is a small bronze plaque which reads:

IN LOVING MEMORY OF
ANNIE DAVIDSON
WHO WAS INSTRUMENTAL IN FOUNDING
THE
CARNEGIE LIBRARY IN CALGARY

ERECTED BY
CALGARY WOMEN'S LITERARY CLUB
1911

Mrs. Davidson lived in Calgary for a few of the early years of this century. She was a woman of culture and refinement, deeply interested in literature. On February 9, 1906 she invited some ladies of like mind to meet at her home on Thirteenth Avenue West, and together they formed the Calgary Women's Literary Club. This club still exists today, the oldest women's club in the city of Calgary.

Mrs. Davidson was named the club's Honorary President, and Mrs. George MacDonald became the first President. Working with an outstanding committee, they piloted a growing number

of members that first year through the study of Shakespeare's *King Richard II* . Meetings were held in the Methodist Church, the use of which had been kindly granted by the Reverend Mr. Kerby, and the fee decided upon was twenty-five cents a year.

The financial statement at the end of the season disclosed that there was a membership of twenty-seven, and the funds of the club amounted to the princely sum of six dollars and seventy-five cents. There had been an expenditure of one dollar (probably to the church's caretaker), and the Secretary-Treasurer was requested to deposit the balance of five dollars and seventy-five cents in one of the local banks.

They had unstinting help from many men, especially those connected with Western Canada College, and others whose wives had taken up membership in the club. In the first year or so, lectures were given by the Reverend Dr. MacRae and Mr. Walker, MA, both of Western Canada College, and by the Reverend Mr. Clark of Knox Church, Judge Stuart, and Bishop Pinkham. The public was invited to many of these occasions and responded in good numbers, so there was considerable enrichment to the community. It was not long before there were offers coming in from various would-be lecturers, each of whom had his favourite subject.

From the beginning of her stay in Calgary, Mrs. Davidson had realized the need for this lusty young city to enjoy the benefits of a public library. She and the Women's Literary Club became the driving force behind the move to found such an institution under the provisions of the Carnegie Foundation. When arrangements had been completed whereby some Carnegie funds would be available and a plebiscite set up, the ladies of the Literary Club gave their best efforts, knocking on doors to solicit votes. Calgary in those days was populated largely by working men and their families, and many of the men were opposed to anything associated with Andrew Carnegie because they believed he ran a "sweat shop". The task was not an easy one, but the club's efforts were

well rewarded when the vote on the library was in the affirmative and the way was cleared for the exciting project.

In 1910, Mrs. Davidson's son, with whom she lived, was transferred back East, and she left with him. She had loved her life in Calgary, and the Literary Club had been a source of pride and joy for the four years she was associated with it. There are in the records of the club, in the Glenbow Archives, two beautiful letters that she wrote to the members. In one she said, "I cannot accustom myself to the thought of leaving the West, where all my interests have identified themselves with the rush and the impetus and the rapid development which are not to be found in the East. I shall miss many a friend and many a habit of the cheery, stimulating western life so congenial to me." Not very long after her arrival in Winnipeg she died, but two years later the library for which she had laboured came to fruition.

The Literary Club wished to honour the memory of this beloved and valued member in some substantial way, and agreed upon a tablet to hang in the new library. They decided that the plaque should be brass, heavy, solid, and mounted with letters of black enamel. They applied to Mr. D.E. Black, Calgary's best known jeweller, for assistance.

The official opening of the library was held on February 27, 1912, at four in the afternoon. Dr. MacRae spoke a few words in commemoration of Mrs. Davidson, and Mrs. MacDonald unveiled the tablet in the presence of the members of the Literary Club and their guests, who included three particular friends of Mrs. Davidson.

A sentence from one of her own letters is a fine way in which to end this little tribute. "God has given me His best gifts in my old age," Annie Davidson wrote, "the gifts of love and joy and an outlook towards the sunrise that grows brighter as I draw nearer to this life's boundary line."

Foster's Cartage

by Kathleen Hymas

Kathleen (Foster) Hymas is the author of Akokiniskway, a history of Rosebud, Alberta, and for a number of years has been the genealogist for the Calgary branch of the United Empire Loyalists.

Born in 1906, the summer her parents arrived in Alberta, Kathleen spent her first years in the city but following the real estate boom of the early teens, the family moved to a farm near Valleyfield. Her mother insisted that the children return to the city each day for school though, so every morning — regardless of the weather — everyone piled into the Model T for the two-mile drive to the Ogden streetcar line.

Oldtimers are all aware, of course, that the Model T had no self-starter; it had to be cranked. "Mother got to be quite successful by standing on the crank and bearing down with all her weight, but one cold morning it simply wouldn't budge. We were wrapped and muffled in the car, anxious to get going, and no doubt testing the limit of her patience by our nagging, but all of a sudden we were surprised to see her go storming back into the house. Moments later she reappeared with the soup kettle that she had had simmering on the stove. She reached in, tossed out the bone, and poured the hot soup over the motor! That did the trick and we were off."

In the three years prior to the First World War, Calgary was in the midst of the biggest building boom of its then brief history. Because of the nearby sandstone quarries, early Scottish stonemasons were attracted to the city's construction trade, and thousands of their descendants still use the many public buildings erected during that era.

My father's business, Foster Cartage, assisted during that boom. He had come to Alberta during the brutal winter of 1906-07, and quickly decided that homesteading on the prairie was no life for him. He retreated into Calgary to establish the King Edward Stables. When the city's steady growth hit full stride in 1911, Dad's horses were put into service hauling away the debris from the many excavations being carved out by manual labor.

Wagon loads of gravel were carted away and used to build approaches for the soon-to-be-constructed Centre Street Bridge, but since the teamsters had to drive over several blocks of city streets, it was inevitable that spillage would occur. Unfortunately Foster's Cartage was liable when this happened, and often Dad had to appear in court to answer charges. Magistrate Sanders, however, understood that sometimes the means had to be overlooked on the way to the end benefit, and often he dismissed the case.

Many things conspired to cause the boom to bust: the quarries were soon depleted and the necessary manpower was called into service at the outbreak of the First World War. At the end of the war, though, Dad's horses and cartage company were again used — this time to lay gravel for new highways. The Cochrane hill, with its steep curves, was a menace and had to be rebuilt twice, but Dad lived long enough to take part in the construction of modern highways and finally even airport runways.

Below: *Teams and wagons of Foster's Cartage haul away debris from the excavation for the new Hudson's Bay Company building in 1911. The shed in the rear background of the picture housed Foster's offices.*

Thomas Valentine, Pioneer

as told to Edith Hunter

Edith Hunter was born in Manitoba but came to Calgary in 1933 to be married. She wrote feature stories for the Herald. *In the late 1930s she moved to Edmonton where she continued her writing, and then, following the Second World War, returned to Calgary. Her story about the Valentine family was based on information given to her by Llew Valentine.*

History teems with tales of explorers who came to this western land in its early days, and lived among the buffalo and Indians. Just as courageous, and generally unsung, were the venturesome souls who came a century later with wives and children, little or no money in their pockets, relying only on their courage and ingenuity to find work. One such adventurer was my father Thomas Valentine, of Dublin, Ireland, who set out for Canada with his wife and six children in September, 1911.

The Ireland of that period was under-industrialized and plagued by crop failures, and was not an ideal place from which to launch six sons into the world. Father pondered over the enthusiastic letters from his good friend Gordon Emerson, who had left Ireland for a remote place in Canada called Calgary, Alberta. He decided to join him. My dad was well equipped to find work in a new and growing city. He had spent seven years as a carpenter's apprentice, and had become a joiner, one skilled in finer and more intricate woodworking. He had also attended Marlborough College, Dublin, studying structural engineering but left before obtaining his qualifying papers.

And so, in the early autumn of 1911, the great adventure for the Valentine family began. I was only five years old at the time, so I remember very little about the sea voyage aboard "The Lake Manitoba". I do recall, however, that after the ship docked at Halifax, we boarded a train which evidently contained colonist cars, because Mother cooked meals for the family on a stove at the end of the car.

On our arrival in Calgary we were welcomed at an establishment called "Immigration Hall", where we were allowed to stay until Father could find suitable accommodation for the family. Although Calgary already had several hotels, these were unsuitable and financially out of reach for most people arriving with large families. There was only one house for rent in the whole of

Calgary at this time, and it was a one-roomed affair, so we were forced to do what many other new arrivals did. Dad bought us a huge tent. We pitched it close to where the zoo is now located, and where there was a whole colony of tent-dwellers. All of us were forced to live this way until we could find or build other accommodation.

Before leaving Dublin, Father, with great foresight, had built several very large trunks, which Mother had packed with warm clothing, bedding and small household needs, not knowing whether any of these staples would be available in the wilds of Canada. So our life in a tent was more comfortable for us than for many families.

For many newcomers, life in Calgary began in a tent. In spite of rustic conditions the family pictured here, decked out in Sunday-best finery, was well prepared to meet their new social obligations.

With the family temporarily housed, Father went looking for a permanent home. But what he, and many like him, did not realize was that frontier cities such as Calgary, contained not only honest newcomers, anxious to make a good life for their families, but many shady characters as well, ready to take advantage of newcomers. One of these predators managed to sell Father some property on an eroding cliff overlooking the Bow River, totally unsuitable for building anything. Subsequently a sign advertising "Tom Campbell's Hats" was erected there, and dominated the landscape for many years.

Later we acquired a couple of lots on Twenty-fourth Avenue Northwest, near the corner of Sixth Street. This area, we were told, was about to become a very fine residential district, although at the time there was no sign of human habitation excepting a farm to the north. There was also no water because the water main stopped at Sixth Street. However, with the help of my oldest brother Bert, and his friend Gordon Emerson, Father put his years as carpenter's apprentice to good use and built the family a substantial bungalow.

Having solved the housing problem, Mother and Father lost no time in attending to their sons' moral training. They joined the congregation of the Anglican Cathedral, (in those days called the Pro-Cathedral), and enrolled five of us boys in the choir, Bert choosing instead to become a scout master. Being a choirboy wasn't an easy life. On Sundays we set out from home on foot, with well-brushed hair and starched Eton collars, for the eleven o'clock service. Dean Paget, at that time in charge of the Cathedral, would invite us to lunch so we could attend Sunday School in the afternoon. After Sunday School we walked home, had dinner, and returned for the evening service. We also had two choir practices during the week.

The hardship in those days was taken for granted. I well remember my early days at King George School when my teacher, Miss MacKenzie, not only had to teach the three Rs, but stoked the school furnace as well.

Thomas Valentine's decision to emigrate was a happy one. He prospered and subsequently held many important positions in Calgary. He was Building Inspector, and Acting City Engineer although he hadn't stayed at Marlborough College quite long enough to get his papers. One of his early enterprises was building the first chapel in the Pro-Cathedral, which was situated over the choir loft. Later, in the early 1930s, he supervised the construction of the Glenmore Dam. He had come a long way from those tent-dwelling days along the Bow River and I'm sure he would have said the journey had been worthwhile.

Mrs. H. H. Sharples

by Kathleen Snow

Kathleen M. Snow, BA, MA, BEd, BLS, was born in Calgary of parents who had arrived in Alberta in 1912 to work with the CPR. For twenty years Kay Snow worked with the Calgary Public Library, and later helped the School Board set up libraries within the system. From 1964 to 1979 she directed a programme of instruction for teacher/librarians at the University of Calgary.

As a young girl Mrs. Snow had accompanied her mother, who was a singer, to concerts at the Calgary Women's Musical Club and met Mrs. Sharples on those occasions.

For over thirty years, musical circles in Calgary benefited from the knowledge, commanding presence and energy of Mrs. Herman Hooper Sharples.

Born Jeanette Smith in Victoria, Australia in 1875, the eleventh of twelve children, she received a musical education, and at the early age of fifteen performed professionally on the stage of the musical theatre. When only sixteen, Jeanette went on tour with a comic opera company, and, in Melbourne, met Mr. Sharples, a representative of a business based in the United States. Eventually they married and their wedding trip was a tour round the world. Subsequently they settled in the New England states, but a visit to Banff in the Rockies made them realise the possibilities in Canada. They chose Calgary as their home and arrived in 1912 with their son Eric. The newcomers attended the first Calgary Exhibition and Stampede that year and were exhilarated with the week's activities.

Mrs. Sharples, beautifully dressed in her best suit, hat and gloves, made her way to the first meeting of the Calgary Women's Musical Club in 1913. There she encountered Mrs. Roland Winter, swathed in purple veils and wearing a toque decorated with artificial violets. The two formidable ladies of the theatre immediately recognized each other's qualities. Mrs. Winter said, "Well, who are you?" Undaunted, Mrs. Sharples soon took office in the club and became president, an office she held for several terms. Eventually she was named Honorary President.

In addition, during those early years, Mrs. Sharples, because of her valuable experience, took part in the spirited local productions of the works of Gilbert and Sullivan. During the First World War she knitted for the troops overseas. Tragically, it was as she was presiding at a benefit

concert for the war effort that she received a telegram saying that her only son had been killed. Putting her grief aside, with iron will and superb poise, she carried on with the concert.

The Calgary Women's Musical Club (later renamed Calgary Musical Club to accommodate male members) was a most important stimulus to the musical life in Calgary. After the war, the ladies met on the mezzanine floor of the Palliser Hotel. The gold, white and blue setting was a perfect background for the fashionable dress of the members who wore elaborate hats with matching accessories. Informality was definitely not the order of the day.

The programme often consisted of a study paper on a composer, and was illustrated with performances of the works discussed. For example, Mrs. T.M. Allen talked about the works of the French composer Cecile Chaminade and sang her songs. As president, Mrs. Sharples introduced the annual meeting which was devoted to the study of local composers and their compositions. This provided a valuable opportunity for the public to hear performances of works by such people as Leonard Leacock and G. Benbow. In addition, she often arranged informal evenings in her home with local composers. Her high standards set the tone for these musical activities.

As resident secretary for the Royal Schools of Music in England, Mrs. Sharples was in a position to be of great assistance to aspiring musicians. The death of her son intensified her interest in young people, and she was tireless in her efforts for their welfare. She enjoyed entertaining the young choristers from St. Stephen's Church, and at times the examinations for the Royal Schools were held in her home where her Steinway piano was at the service of the students.

The Women's Musical Club was an important stimulus to musical life in Calgary. Patrons, gathered at the old Corral in 1926 for a Galli Curci recital, sit in rapt attention on kitchen chairs. Did they bring their own?

Her connections in the world of music were wide, as she entertained most of the visiting musical celebrities in her home, and charmed them with her wit, sophistication and imposing presence. Such world figures as Jascha Heifetz, Rachmaninoff, Richard Crooks, Galli Curci, Fritz Kreisler and Sir Ernest MacMillan became her friends.

All facets of musical life in Calgary came under the kindly but shrewd eye of Mrs. H.H. Sharples. She and her husband were active supporters of the Provincial Musical Festival; Mr. Sharples held office in the organizing committees. In the small, homogeneous Calgary of those days, the excitement generated by the competition between large church choirs or the solo competition for the Stutchbury Cup was city wide. Mrs. Sharples was on more than one occasion chosen to present the trophies.

The Second World War curtailed many of the cultural activities, but the Musical Club carried on. Mrs. Sharples continued as Honorary President, but much of her time was again devoted to knitting the hundreds of mitts, socks, and scarves that would be sent to the Canadian forces.

After the war, the Allied Arts Council was organized and Mrs. Sharples became the first life member. The Sharples collection of oriental treasures hung on the walls of the renovated Coste House. In 1955 she was given the Distinguished Citizen's Award, and at that time she reminisced about the cultural life of early Calgary. She lived to be ninety-one, alert, interested and as memorable a character as Calgary has ever known.

One Woman Alone

by Ruth Gorman

Part of the attraction of the western frontier must surely have been its open-handed acceptance of strong-willed adventurers. People willing to work hard and share the labour as well as the rewards of the new province were welcomed as pioneers — race nor creed was neither help nor hindrance. And even though the Jewish people, uprooted from European homelands, brought little but an ancient heritage, they soon won the appreciation of their new neighbours in Alberta and enriched the province by untold measure. Such an immigrant was Bella Singer.

In 1907, Abraham Singer, Bella's husband, fled a troubled Poland to seek a new start in Canada. Within two years he sent for his wife, and Bella boarded the steamship for the long trip to the New World. She spoke not a word of English, she had no money or education, but she *was* accustomed to hard work. In Winnipeg, Bella and her husband sold goods from door to door until they could afford to come to Calgary. There was no welcome committee to meet them, and Calgary itself was a rather drab, bleak town set in the midst of the treeless prairie, but to Bella this tolerant city looked just fine. It was the beginning of her dream to obtain for her own family what she called another chance.

Her husband first had a job with the railroad, and Bella ran one of the railway's many boarding houses. The hard work didn't bother her, but she felt constant guilt about the family and friends she had left behind in Europe. One day her employer told her that the CPR would bring an immigrant over to Calgary if she could pay 150 dollars cash and would guarantee that he would have care and employment once he arrived. That was the beginning.

She not only raised her own four children and ran the boarding house, but she then began working nights cleaning offices and other boarding houses. Bella had no education, but she was clever enough to choose a young lawyer to advise her on the contract and to write the necessary immigration letters. His name was R.B. Bennett. Later he would become Prime Minister of Canada, as well as Bella's friend and legal adviser.

The first Jewish immigrant she brought to Calgary was Charlie Switzer. She took him into her boarding house and found him employment. All she asked in return was that he would pay the way of another immigrant, who in turn would pay for another. Bella understood the principle of the pyramid. Soon the boarding house was bursting at the seams and another had to be acquired as the number of new arrivals increased. Eventually even a small hotel was purchased.

Many now-prominent Calgarians, like the Belzburg family, owe their success stories to Bella's human lifeline. It is suspected that over three hundred people found another chance through Bella's help, but ironically, even though Sucher Cyngiser was plucked from Hitler's Germany, Bella could not save her own two sisters from the holocaust.

On her seventieth birthday hundreds of those to whom she had given another chance for life attended her party. It was held in the ballroom of the CPR's Palliser Hotel, the very company whose boarding house she had once cleaned to turn her dream into a reality. She had had no education and she had worried that Calgary had no rabbi, but Mrs. Singer lived long enough to have the Holy Ark of the Shaarey Tzedec congregation dedicated in her honour. She had had nothing but a driving ability to work hard, a faith in the future of her new home and a desire to share her good fortune. And now, all Calgary is in her debt.

Bella and Abraham Singer and their family, 1919. Many now-prominent Calgarians owe their success stories to Bella's human lifeline.

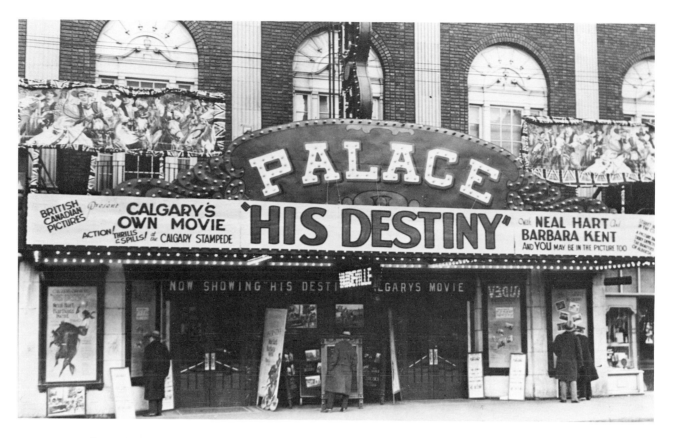

The Palace Theatre was host to "His Destiny", Calgary's own movie. This Stampede thriller was filmed in the 1920s on Guy Weadick's ranch and many Calgarians were featured as extras. The Palace was heralded in the '20s as a deluxe theatre. Chandeliers, heavy velvet draperies and Grecian pilasters were all a part of the expected decor in the big movie theatres of the day. Even today, the Palace still functions as a theatre for occasional musical productions.

Going to the Movies

by Frances Coulson

Frances Coulson was born in Ottawa in 1905 and came to Calgary seven years later when her doctor father began his medical practice in this city. After attending university, *Mrs. Coulson became the librarian at the Alexander Calhoun branch, but her obvious love for "the movies" makes her a special authority of the history of Calgary theatres.*

Going to the movies on Saturday afternoon was a popular pastime for Calgary's young fry in the years between 1912 and 1919. The screens were small, the films were all in black and white and, if they happened to be old, cracks and specks made it look like falling rain. The actors spoke — at least their lips moved — but what they were supposed to have said appeared on subtitles. The action of those silent films was interpreted by the frantic accompaniment of a lone piano player, plus enthusiastic audience participation. There was no lobby sale of soft drinks or popcorn; we brought our own candy. Peanuts were considered bad form and bag rattling was frowned upon.

Two of our favourites among Calgary's early movie houses were the Globe on the south side of Eighth Avenue, east of Centre Street, and the Regent on Eighth Avenue where the Bay now stands. Admission was ten cents and when the Great War started, a war tax of one cent was collected. There were no intermissions between the one and two-reel pictures — unless the film broke or the operator had trouble changing reels.

Cowboy and Indian pictures were favourites. The cowboy was usually involved in rescuing a pretty girl, and invariably both would take shelter behind an immense rock. From this vantage point the hero, with blazing gun, would decimate the attacking Indians while showers of arrows fell harmlessly around him.

People liked comedies too. Charlie Chaplin was known as the little tramp and appeared regularly in those one-reelers. There were hilarious chases by the Keystone Cops and lively comedies involving the Mack Sennett Bathing Beauties.

As time went on, movies began to get longer, and three-reelers weren't uncommon. Once a five-reel movie came to Calgary's elegant Sherman Grand, which had opened in 1912 as a legitimate stage theatre. The film featured Annette Kellerman in "Neptune's Daughter." The actress was a noted swimmer and audiences were thrilled (and shocked) when she was shown in the distance clad in white tights. Although she was covered from neck to ankles, this was considered to be extremely daring!

In 1914 a new movie theatre opened a short distance from the Globe. The Allen boasted seats upholstered in crimson plush and, if memory doesn't fail, an organ. Here we saw such pictures as "Tess of the Storm Country" with Mary Pickford and "Snowwhite and the Seven Dwarfs" with Marguerite Clark. The star system was beginning and we all had our favourites; Mary Pickford of course, led the list. The handsome Wally Reid was the heart throb of the day and Francis X. Bushman, famed for his noble profile, stirred our youthful passions. Lillian and Dorothy Gish were much admired and the bouncy, athletic Douglas Fairbanks had his following.

The introduction of the movie serial greatly enhanced attendance at the Saturday matinees. We returned week after week to see the death-defying hero or heroine escaping, or being rescued from cliff-hanging, drowning, falling into mine shafts, being tied to railroad tracks, severed by buzz-saws or torn asunder by wild animals. There was one blood-curdling movie called "Lucille Love, the Girl of Mystery" which must have run for at least a year. However, we were forced to

forego the "Perils of Pauline" because it was shown at the Pantages Theatre, a vaudeville house considered to be too sophisticated for our young minds.

About 1915, David Wark Griffith's epoch-making "Birth of a Nation" appeared. Because it was reputed to have cost a million dollars, admission prices were raised to one dollar, so *this* movie fan had to wait twenty years before seeing it!

There were, of course, other theatres: the Empress, the Bijou and the Isis. The Isis was on First Street West at Twelfth Avenue. But it was a great day when our neighbourhood movie, the Royal, opened at Fourteenth Street and Seventeenth Avenue in 1914. We became instant patrons. Since it was within walking distance (streetcar tickets cost a quarter for ten!) we could afford to spend a nickel for a chocolate bar. Years later, the Royal was refurbished and became the Kinema.

The Princess, on the north side of Eighth Avenue, east of what is now the Macleod Trail, opened with great fanfare in 1914. Between films a young *Herald* paper boy named Scotty Johnson came onstage and sang "I'm on my Way to Mandalay" in a ringing boyish tenor. The second verse of the song went: "I want to go, to Mexico / Beneath the Stars and Stripes to fight for the foe." At the conclusion of the song Scotty pulled out an American flag and waved it, and that just brought down the house!

The Allen Palace and the Capitol opened in the 1920s. They were deluxe theatres seating large audiences who were led to their seats by smartly uniformed ushers. As teenagers, we sighed over stunning Latin lovers like Rudolph Valentino, Ramon Navarro and John Gilbert. The large theatres employed orchestras to create appropriate moods to accompany the films' action and they also played during intermissions. But a new development at the end of the '20s was to put an end to both the movie orchestras and the whole world of silent film. The talkies spoke ruin for many of the stars of silent days, as well as the whole technique of silent movie-making. It was the end of an era, even though, for me at least, the magic memory lingers on.

The Empire Theatre was affiliated with the Pantages circuit, a vaudeville house considered to be too sophisticated for "our" young minds.

Facing Page: *The death-defying escapades of heros, like Two Fisted Jones, kept a generation of Calgarians in cliff-hanging suspense at the Empress Theatre.*

Getting Around

by Betty Burns

Betty Burns is the daughter of David E. Black, who owned an early Calgary jewelry store. Born and raised in a house on Seventeenth Avenue, she has fond memories of the young city. She was educated at Mount Royal School, St. Hilda's and Western Canada High School and graduated with a B.A. from the University of Alberta. Interested in journalism, she worked at the Herald for a few years before her marriage.

Black's jewelry store, a landmark of pioneer Calgary now located at Heritage Park, can still be seen today. But much of the rest of early Calgary, including Betty Burns' Musical Sight-Seeing Street Car, has long vanished.

From the very beginning my father had trouble with his brand-new, bright red, open-air Franklin Roadster. In those days the automobile was a novelty in Calgary, and this particular vehicle was more than a challenge to its new owner.

The car, it seems, couldn't be controlled. It reacted more like a high-spirited horse than an accumulation of mechanical parts, and apparently it had become commonplace for sidewalk pedestrians to see Dad, on any given morning, go streaming east on Seventeenth Avenue with all valves open! Unintentionally, of course.

One earnest member of the law enforcement branch suggested that a judicious use of the brake might be a solution to the high-speed monster. One can only guess what he thought about the capabilities of the operator of the vehicle, but evidently those opinions didn't transfer, because not much later came an official warning: "Slow down, or else!" And then came that Saturday of infamy. Struggling with this unruly machine of questionable personality, it was with great misgivings that Dad saw a uniformed policeman step out from the curb at First Street Southwest, and, with arm raised, bring him to a halt.

"Morning, Mr. Black. I'm selling tickets for the Police Benefit Dance next Saturday, and wondered if you and Mrs. Black would like to come?"

Dad bought the entire book of tickets on the spot. It had been a close shave, though I doubt his enthusiasm for his car was dampened in the slightest.

For me, though, there was a vehicle far more exciting than Father's car. When I was a child, I used to stand on the sidewalk outside our home to watch with excitement as the Spanking White,

Mr. Black, undoubtedly a fan of Stampede Week Auto Racing, was, like the many citizens gathered here,
fascinated by the technological wonder of the new century.

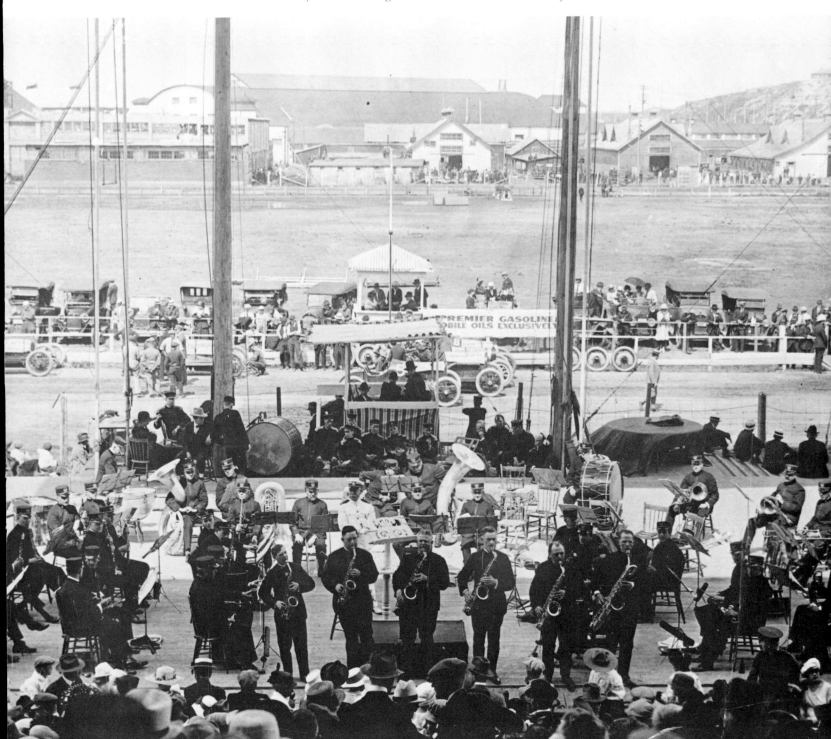

Speed held a great attraction for most early Calgarians. In the picture above, participants in a 1911 auto race thrill their onlookers. Below, a roadster converted to sports car style is parked outside Central Park Library. The practice of modifying cars for both street and race track was common in the teens.

Facing Page: The Spanking-White, Mirror-Sided, Musical, Sightseeing Street Car, Calgary's glittering transportation queen. If you were lucky you could see a contorted image of yourself reflected in those shimmering, sparkling mirrors as it passed.

Mirror-Sided, Musical Sight-Seeing Street Car approached up our hill.

It was an open-air trolley with seats tiered upward from front to back. A lively melody played on the calliope, while the conductor announced the sights worth attention over a hand-held megaphone. Of course he had to shout to make himself heard over the music and quite frequently he came second.

But the exquisite thrill came as the streetcar passed by close to where I stood, because, if I was lucky, I could see a contorted image of myself reflected in those shimmering, sparkling mirrors. All out of proportion, passing too quickly, but I knew it was me waving when the image waved back! And so did most of the passengers on that fairyland street car.

I never did have a ride, even to Bowness Park, on that glittering transportation queen, but I think that that deprivation probably made the wonderful chariot still more enchanting.

Wings for a Cowtown

by Tom Moore

Old-time pilots — the kind who used to fly by the seat of their pants rather than by instruments — often claimed they could fly a kitchen table if they had enough power to get it aloft. That was the main trouble with early attempts to fly in Calgary: there wasn't enough power available. But it was only three years after the Wright brothers took off in a heavier-than-air machine at Kitty Hawk, North Carolina, that a pair of young Calgarians attempted to emulate the feat.

They didn't quite make it.

J. Earle Young and Alf Lauder put a tremendous amount of effort into building a glider, and they got it into the air when they towed it behind an automobile. Many, many times they gained an altitude of fifteen to twenty feet and the dream of flying seemed to be within their grasp. Then they installed a one-cylinder motor — but that was too much for the glider. It never did get off the ground under its own power. The engine was too heavy, and the amount of power it produced was too little.

You can still get an argument over who actually made the first airplane flight in Calgary

Captain McCall had, by 1918, shot down thirty-seven enemy aircraft and two balloons, so stunt flying in Calgary — no matter how hairy the emergency landings — was pretty tame stuff to the war hero.

CAPT. F.R. McCALL DSO M.C. BAR D.F.C.

— and in what kind of an airplane. The honour was claimed on July 3, 1911, by a barnstorming exhibition aviator named Howard Le Van who thrilled a grandstand full of people at the Calgary Exhibition with a flight around the race track in a flimsy biplane with a pusher propeller. The flight has often been called the "first" in Calgary, mainly because Mr. Le Van said it was — and besides being a pioneer aviator, old timers said that Mr. Le Van was a great ballyhoo artist who could deliver as fine a spiel as any veteran talker on a midway side show.

It may be, however, that Mr. Le Van's claim was genuine — the city limits being where they were in 1910 — because the other top challenger for the honour actually made his flight at Shouldice Park, a few miles up the Bow River from Calgary. He was a man named Simmer, and he came from Chicago in 1910 and found an enthusiastic partner for a plane building enterprise in J. Gordon Mackie of Calgary.

Simmer, who had gained some experience in aircraft building in the United States and who worked as a mechanic in Calgary, spent many months building a plane with the help of young Mackie in a barn on Fifth Avenue East. It was a Curtiss-type biplane, powered by a forty-horsepower Maxim motor, and it could stay up in the air for half an hour when Simmer made some flights in it at Shouldice. The machine was taken to Coronation for exhibition flights and crashed — but it was a low-altitude crash and nobody was seriously hurt. The plane was repaired and made many more exhibition flights in the years before the First World War.

In 1913 a French pilot, Didier Mason, flew a Farman machine with a Gnome engine in exhibition flights at the Calgary fair, and another exhibition headliner — Kathryn Stinson — was the first woman to fly in the city. She flew in 1916 and also carried the first unofficial airmail between Calgary and Edmonton.

When the Great War was over, aces who had fought in the skies of France returned to

The '20s roared in Calgary as new-fangled air ships buzzed awe-struck spectators at the Renfrew air show.

Old-time pilots used to brag they could fly the kitchen table if only they had enough power to get it aloft. In this 1930 photo, pilot/builder Hugh C. Johnson stands proudly by his Pietenpol air camper, which he powered by a Ford Model A engine.

When the Great War was over, Ace Freddie McCall returned to Calgary and started writing a new chapter in the history of aviation. Here he refuels his Stinson from a Regal Gasoline truck.

Canada and started to write a new chapter in the history of aviation — with Calgary's Captain Fred McCall, DSO, MC and bar, DFC well to the fore.

It was McCall, who had shot down thirty-seven enemy aircraft and two balloons early in 1918, who walked away from one of Calgary's most spectacular crashes. Stunt-flying at the Calgary Exhibition in 1919, he took off from centre field of the race track on a brief sightseeing flip with the two young sons of exhibition manager E.L. Richardson. The machine failed to gain speed and Captain McCall had his choice of crashing into racing autos on the race track or into the midway. He figured he could find a little empty space on the latter. Heading over the fence, he hit a telephone pole. From that he caromed to the top of the merry-go-round. By some miracle, there he stuck, and nobody was hurt.

In 1918, an experimental airmail service was operated out of Calgary, and many claimed it was unique in the world. Planes flew between Calgary and Winnipeg with no navigational aids, and, in 1920, regular service was started. In the experimental days, the pilots "felt" their way into the city and it is on record that A.H. Farrington, Western Canada Airways pilot, once was delayed so much by headwinds that he was given up for lost — but finally brought his machine to land. It was long after dark, he had no lights to guide him and no instruments for that kind of flying. Yet he stopped only a few feet from the shed that served as a hangar at the Calgary airport, which at that time was just behind Stanley Jones School on the North Hill.

H. Hollick Kenyon carried the first official airmail in 1930 in a Boeing biplane; Pat Holden crashed at Gleichen with two passengers as he tried to get the mail through in September fog the same year, and pilots fought through mountain passes late in the '30s to extend the service. It was a great era of flying — and Calgary was in the thick of it.

A Grumman Goose on display at the Renfrew airport during the 1931 Trans-Canada Air Pageant.

Days of My Childhood

by Allan Anderson

Allan Anderson, an oral historian and senior Canadian writer, is the editor of Roughnecks and Wildcatters, *an account of the early oil industry in western Canada. Mr. Anderson grew up in Calgary and his recollections here are about the city* as he remembers and loves it. As he says, "If there is one place you will find great, great storytellers, it's Calgary. Go for the lively, personal stuff, what I call 'grass-roots history' and you will have a glorious story."

My very first memory of Calgary is the end of the Great War, November 11th, 1918. I can remember vaguely the newsboys running through the streets, shouting loudly, and selling the special edition of the paper.

We lived in a stucco bungalow at the corner of Nineteenth Avenue and Fourth Street. It was a pleasant, residential part of Calgary. I think there's a gas station there now! My sister and I had twin beds in a small room on the second floor. I would lie in bed and, just before I fell asleep, watch with delight the reflection of the lights of cars race across the ceiling above my head.

There had been a tennis court on the land my father bought for the house. Prior to that, it had been virgin prairie. The earth was so hard my father couldn't break it up for a garden. He was determined to have one though, so he made little holes with a pickaxe and put cut-up bits of potatoes in them. The potatoes grew to the size of footballs – I have never since seen anything like them – they loosened the soil beautifully. Soon, vegetables and flowers abounded.

My father planted a hedge of caragana, a hearty and very tough Siberian shrub. It was as thick and solid as a brick wall, a magnificent hedge facing the street. Another street came in at right angles, meeting the street along which the hedge ran. One day, a car came down this street and smashed head-on into the hedge. The front of the car was bashed in, but the caragana suffered little injury and just stood there, sneering at the car.

We had most congenial neighbours to the left of our house, as you faced it. They were the Harmons and they were American. My sister and I used to play with their two children. I could never get over one peculiarity about the Harmons. Amongst other foods, they ate apple pie for breakfast. This entranced me. Who had ever heard of anyone eating apple pie for breakfast?

My mother was terrified of her own shadow and given to tantrums. Terrible dust-storms

Judge and Lady Winter's house had big trees and that kind of forest gloom you find in long-settled estates in eastern Canada.

descended on Calgary. The world would be obliterated. There was no way of keeping the dust out of the house. It would filter in, covering everything. The gritty sand would get in your lungs. In the darkened rooms, my mother, a fastidious housekeeper, would become hysterical. This only intensified the ominous presence of the sand-storm for my sister and myself.

Across the street from us was one of Calgary's most charming estates. It was the home of Judge and Lady Winter. As I recall it, she was always referred to as "Lady Winter". There were big trees and that kind of forest gloom you find in long-settled estates in eastern Canada. I could never figure out how those great trees had grown so quickly on the prairies. The Winters had a bowling green, and this, of course, was another marvel for a small boy.

Lady Winter was unique. The story was that she had been born on a British battleship in Shanghai harbour, the daughter of an English diplomat. There were a number of eccentric British characters around Calgary in those days, Lady Winter foremost amongst them.

Lady Winter could be a grande dame indeed, wearing a huge hat and a handsome gown. She was interested in the arts and, so I understood, started the Little Theatre movement in Calgary. However, there was another side to Lady Winter. She could put on an old beat-up gown that I thought was gingham and pad around in her bare feet in her garden. She adored gardening.

Her husband, Judge Winter, was a pleasant, ineffectual character, who, my father told me, was given to such inanities as driving down the wrong side of the street when the fire wagons were rushing right at him. In his courtroom, he was invariably polite to everyone.

Judge Winter tried to help his wife in the garden by pulling weeds. Most of his time, unfortunately, was spent yanking up Lady Winter's prize flowers. Lady Winter had a dazzling command of curses and oaths and, to this day, I can still hear her bawling out her poor husband in language that would have horrified anyone but a pioneer western woman. Lady Winter impressed me greatly. As I look back on her now, her high style and her earthy bawdiness embodied the best of the old West.

Sometimes it would be fifty below zero Fahrenheit, but it was a dry cold and not bone-chilling. If one's nose was freezing and turning white, a passerby would point to it and the nose would get a brisk rubbing to stir up the circulation.

My father walked to work and back every day. He was City Passenger Agent for the CPR. Once he went thirteen years without taking a holiday and he would even drop in at the office on Sundays. The CPR, a hard-nosed and ruthless corporation, expected this kind of dedication from its employees and wouldn't have dreamed of thanking them for it.

My father came from Chatham, New Brunswick, where R.B. Bennett had his first law practice. They both went to Calgary about the same time. My father was rector's warden at St. Stephen's Church. One day he was talked into asking Bennett for a contribution towards a new church steeple. My father was a courteous gentleman but shy about soliciting donations. However, there was no way out. Bennett welcomed him heartily and gave him five dollars. It took all my father's courage to go back to the church with this meagre contribution. I hated Bennett ever afterwards. I met Bennett later, with my father, and found him a big, red-faced, domineering, unlikable man.

I was born in Calgary in 1915, and I have very fond memories of what I insist in thinking of as a friendly little cowtown. Actually, Calgary had fifty-five thousand people in 1912, the year of the first Stampede, and was roaring ahead. Even so, it had a congenial neighbourly atmosphere. I think I thought of it as a cowtown because, during the Stampede parade, real cowboys off the range would be roping good-looking girls on the street. I knew they were real cowboys and they were my heroes.

In 1925, my father moved up the ladder from City Passenger Agent to an executive position with the CPR in Montreal. My poor mother's pride at his promotion was deflated completely when *The Calgary Herald* ran a story headed "City Gassenger Agent Promoted."

Boy! What a Ride!

by Grace Shaw

Grace (Lydiatt) Shaw was born in Calgary, and grew up in an atmosphere of music and the arts. Her father R. Jeffery Lydiatt, as vice-president of Trans-Canada Theatres, was responsible for booking touring companies into Canadian theatres. Mrs. Shaw's career has embraced broadcasting, writing, merchandising, design, advertising and public relations in cities all over North America. Her CBC radio programmes have been extensive and her thirteen-week series, Canadian Theatre — Fact or Fancy, *encompassed research and interviews from every province in Canada. Mrs. Shaw has recently prepared* Stratford Under Cover *in honour of the twenty fifth season of the Stratford Festival, but in celebration of her hometown reminisces here about Calgary.*

Forty-two children lived on Eleventh Street West in the early 1920s, all in one block, between Seventeenth and Nineteenth Avenues South. Four of them were Browns, the offspring of Mr. and Mrs. R.A. Brown, and six of us were Lydiatts. The families, needless to say, were close friends.

Sleighriding was the favourite winter sport in that neighbourhood, and we children had the best hill in town, right at our doorstep. It went straight up from Nineteenth all the way to Prospect, so when the snow was packed down hard, the sleighs went lickity-split. The best ride though was on a bobsled and not everybody had one of those.

Neil Brown had the great good fortune to find a sleigh under the Christmas tree one year. His pal, Ellis Lydiatt, already had one, and, since two sleighs and a plank were all they needed to make a bobsled, we knew that soon we would be in for high adventure. Somewhere they found a plank but how they managed to lug it home was anyone's guess; it was sixteen feet long!

The two boys worked most of the day while all the kids on the street watched in eager anticipation. They fastened one end of the plank securely to Neil's sleigh on the front. It had the best steering bar. By bolting the plank to the front sleigh, the driver could manipulate the bobsled.

By dinnertime the super-sled was ready. Everyone begged to be on the first ride but Neil and Ellis decided to take their sisters and brothers. Ellis tried to persuade Mrs. Brown to take a ride and much to his delight she accepted. She was a large woman and her weight was just what was needed for a faster ride.

The night was cold and clear with well packed snow. Barriers at Nineteenth Avenue kept the cars away, and the fireman at the station on the corner of Seventeenth Avenue had spread ashes on the road to slow us down. The street took a jog at that corner and a speeding bobsled could go right across the streetcar tracks.

The bigger boys pulled the bobsled up the long hill while the rest of us chattered excitedly as we climbed on foot. Finally we were at Prospect Avenue.

Ellis was to steer. He lay on his stomach, hands gripping both handles of the bar. The rest of us sat holding onto the legs of the child behind, with Mrs. Brown taking up her position at the rear.

One good push and we were off! The farther we went, the faster we went, all of us screaming with glee! Mrs. Brown was pale and silent. By the time we crossed Nineteenth Avenue we were almost flying! Only one flat block to go before the bobsled would come to the ashes.

Neighbours and parents were watching the speeding sled with the riders shouting and waving as it swooshed by. Past the firehall and right through the ashes it went. Across Seventeenth Avenue. The cartracks. Up over the sidewalk. And smack into the basement window of the Chinese laundry!

The glee changed to astonishment. Mrs. Brown had fallen off the back and the laundryman shook his fists, shouting in Chinese. Slowly Ellis pulled his head out of the window, forehead bleeding, but he had a big grin on his face as he turned to the others, "Boy! What a Ride!"

When you had forty-two children to a block it wasn't hard to scare up a team for what-ever you wanted to play. This robust group of children get ready for a hockey game.

Bobsleds were made by joining two runner-sleighs with a plank whose length was
determined only by the courage of its intended riders. This little boy and his babysitter
opted for a modest eight-footer.

99

The Remarkable Mrs. Jones

by Eva Reid

Eva Reid began her career after training at Mount Royal College, and "tumbled into" journalism at the end of the Depression. She at first wrote for the Social Credit Journal *and later for the* Calgary Albertan *where she became one of the first women in Canada to become a provincial editor. Covering both women's issues and magistrates' court, she often said that her two most frequently used reference books were* Emily Post *and the* Criminal Code.

In November of 1978 the University of Calgary conferred a Master's degree in Canadian history on May Jones. Fifty-eight years had passed since her undergraduate convocation at King's College, and a lifetime of honours had followed her through changing careers.

Scarcely five feet tall, May began her education seemingly unaware of the current prejudices against women, but certainly she stood taller than the small minds that rejected a woman in a "man's" field. In 1920 she graduated with degrees in science and engineering however, and to her surprise was offered a job in Halifax with a mining firm. Her gratitude was short-lived, though, when she realized that she had been hired as girl Friday rather than fellow engineer, so she left to take an education degree. Graduating with a superior first ranking, she departed the confines of the Maritimes and headed west.

Calgary welcomed the young teacher and she began instructing in physics and chemistry at Mount Royal College. She was soon joined by Sidney Jones, a fellow Maritimer, who had also been a King's College engineering graduate unable to obtain a suitable position. They were married in 1922 and May left her teaching position to become a full time homemaker and mother. Then began an active career as a volunteer with the Mount Royal College Education Club, the Symphony and the Engineering Institute of Canada. Mrs. Jones co-founded the Calgary University Women's Club, and fifty years later was honoured for her contributions to the organization.

When the Second World War began and Canadian men left for the European front, there was a resulting shortage of engineers left in Calgary to oversee the developing oil industry. Mrs. Jones offered her services to the Petroleum and Natural Gas Conservation Board. Her talent for the work was immediately evident and she became assistant to the Chief Engineer — a post she held until the late 1940s. Again she retired, explaining, "One of the returning servicemen might

May Jones, pictured here with fellow students at the 1978 University of Calgary convocation, was awarded a Master's degree at the age of seventy-nine. Her thesis was titled The Search for Hydrocarbons: Petroleum and Natural Gas in Western Canada 1883 - 1947.

need the job."   The years passed quickly for the Jones family. Sidney Jones continued his career in the Mathematics Department of Central Collegiate Institute, and May Jones devoted increasing energy to the volunteer projects that demanded her services.

In 1969, however, May's husband died, and in grief she attended a memorial at King's College in his honour. While there, Mrs. Jones confided to the President of the College that she had always intended to do some graduate work in the field of history, but that time had never allowed her to begin serious research. "No time like the present," advised the academic. "When you go back to Calgary, get in touch with Dr. A.W. Rasporich at the University and talk to him about your idea."

The seedling idea blossomed, and her research, which analyzed the oil and gas industry, was eventually titled *The Search for Hydrocarbons: Petroleum and Natural Gas in Western Canada 1883-1947*. Her earlier work with the Energy Conservation Board and her acquaintance and interviews with the pioneers of the industry covered a period for which there had been very little documentation, so her thesis was heartily welcomed by both the academic and petroleum communities. So impressive had her efforts been, she was immediately commissioned to write a sequel embracing the period from 1947 to 1978. Like its precursor, the work is now housed in the National Museum Archives in Ottawa.

May Jones, a pathfinder in the career of life, found opportunity at every roadblock. Never considering herself a second class citizen, she never recognized that her sex may have been an obstacle, but rather viewed her open-ended projects as windows to further interests. Calgary profited by her intelligence, curiosity and enthusiasm, and women of a later generation regarded her as a wonderful role model.

Suddenly, there was an almighty "Whump!" and the derrick became a candle of billowing flame.

102

The Turner Valley Candle

by Jack Peach

One of the fiercest sights of my youth was the burning of an oilwell, called Royalite #4, in the town of Turner Valley. In October, 1924 a drilling crew had struck a good flow of wet gas near the three-thousand-foot level, but oil was the true prize. Just when the backers were about to give up on the venture, it was decided to go a few feet more "just in case".

The drill bit was about forty feet into the limestone formation when, deep under the drilling crews' feet, there were rumblings and belching, enough to make them all scatter before disaster hit. All on its own, out of the hole rose the eight inch pipe, then the six inch pipe, like toothpaste out of a tube, straight into the air, followed by the drill bit. Suddenly there was an almighty "Whump!" and the derrick became a candle of billowing flame.

The fire could be seen fifty miles away, and a pennant of smoke from the blazing naphtha streamed across the sky, attracting people like moths to see the incredible tornado of flame. The drill pipe, towering above the blackened earth, was thick with frost for the first thirty feet, and, for the next twenty feet up, was a slender black column screaming at the skies.

Above the lip of the pipe was a quivering mass of gas capped by a billowing fire that seemed determined to set the heavens alight. And all around, the ground trembled while the air throbbed, and even the crew, striving to put the fire out, seemed suspended in noise.

It took months to tame the well. A battery of steam boilers was set up like a row of

Oil companies' hastily built shack-offices — typical Turner Valley architecture of the 1920s.

103

Turner Valley's pastoral setting was littered with oil derricks by the 1930s.

fat dray horses. The boilers were connected to one another, fired up and, as we watched, a signal was given and on came the steam. It screamed too, but not as loud as the gas from the well. Suddenly, in an enormous cloud of steam, there was no fire. Then the huge outpouring of Royalite #4 was gingerly divided and captured in tanks. What couldn't be trucked away for conversion to gasoline was flared over a bend in Sheep Creek.

That flame played to one more audience, a group of French film makers from Paris led by impressionist painter Paul Coze. The group filmed and sketched some almost forgotten tribal dances performed by a group of local Indians at night against the lurid background.

A "Christmas Tree" of valves still stands in the field in the heart of Turner Valley, a workaday monument to an episode in Alberta's petroleum story.

A Not Quite So Legal Limit

by Jack Scott

Jack Scott was born in 1894 in Australia. He arrived in Alberta with his parents in 1905, and homesteaded with them near Carmangay. Following service in the First World War, Scott returned to Alberta where he worked wielding a hammer and saw for the CPR's bridge and building department, becoming in time a full-fledged carpenter. With this skill he settled in Calgary and began working for the Hay and Harding Cartage Company, producing breadwagons for home delivery routes and closed wagons for laundries. Milk wagons, moving vans and school buses predated the motorized vehicles of a later age, but at Scott's direction the company moved into the modern world. Jack Scott therefore surveys Calgary's progress with the objective eye of a true pioneer, and also recalls the humour and high jinks of the relaxed era of a generation or two ago with the appreciation of a participant.

Nat and Stoney Christie owned the big steam laundry on Fifth Avenue, and they were famous for having fifty of the smartest horse-drawn rigs in the city. And besides that, the boys were expert trap shooters. Stoney was the long time president of the gun club, but I think that Nat might have been the better hunter. Or at least the more clever of the two.

It was opening day for ducks, and Stoney and Nat were on their favourite hunting grounds north of Strathmore. The birds were plentiful and flying low, so the day was young when the brothers were putting their birds into the back of Nat's old Dodge. Their count revealed a few more than the legal limit, and unfortunately Folton, the game warden, appeared and demanded to count the bag. On discovering a few extra birds he proceeded to write out summonses demanding that the culprits appear the following week in the Strathmore court for sentencing.

Nat couldn't see the sense of making an extra trip. "Why not go to the magistrate now and get it over with?" So off they went, Stoney in front driving with Folton beside him, and Nat in the back with the take, next to the open window, allowing air to circulate to keep the birds fresh.

No sooner had Stoney stopped the car in front of the magistrate's office than Folton rushed in to inform him that he had a couple of guys who wanted to pay their fines and get going. The minute they were alone Nat whispered to Stoney, "Plead not guilty."

The magistrate, being as informal as possible, said, "Court is in session. What's the charge?"

"Shooting over the legal number of birds, Your Honour," said Folton.

"Guilty or not?" inquired the magistrate.

"Not guilty," was the prompt reply from the Christie brothers.

"What?" said the magistrate, "Can't you agree on the count? Bring in the evidence!"

When Folton went to the car to get the birds he found that their number was significantly reduced, and, discovering the open window, he was quick to conclude what had happened.

The trial didn't take long. How the game warden got back to his car I never learned, but I doubt that he accepted the hospitality of the Christie brothers.

These turn-of-the-century duck hunters pose with their trophies. Damn poor shots in the days before legal limits!

The Enforcement of Justice in More Gentle Days

by Jack Saucier

J.J. Saucier, QC, began his legal practice after graduation from the faculty of law at the University of Alberta in 1926, and in 1934 Prime Minister R.B. Bennett invited him to accept the position as his assistant private secretary in Ottawa. It was, however, with profound relief that Saucier returned to Calgary the following year to resume his career. He once again began practising with the Bennett firm where he did extensive litigation and corporate work, and in time headed the firm as senior partner.

Since Mr. Saucier's first language is French, as a bilingual representative from the West, his tenure as President of the Canadian Bar Association was a highly successful one. And because he writes (in both languages) as entertainingly as he speaks, his stories about early Calgary courtrooms are told with the skill of a born raconteur.

Alas, what was once a charming railway and wholesale distributing centre has become a modern metropolis, and no longer is the greatly augmented police force regarded with the friendly sentiments of those of a previous generation. No longer is it possible to proffer humble apologies to prosecuting constables.

On one occasion, a highly respectable Scottish executive (in his cups) undertook to intervene in a public place where two uniformed constables were dealing with a minor infraction by an obvious tourist. This led to the prominent gentleman's forcible apprehension.

On the following Monday the accused attended with counsel upon Chief Constable Sam Patterson. Counsel submitted that if his client should be convicted, the punishment would exceed the crime since his client could lose an important executive post. Chief Patterson indicated that under the circumstances he would agree to the withdrawal of the charge only with the consent of both arresting constables. The accused promptly proffered humble apologies to both policemen. One willingly agreed to the withdrawal, but his partner, with a heavy Scottish accent, rumbled, "No God Damn Rotarian from Mount Royal is going to call *me* a flat-footed-Scottish-son-of-a-

bitch and get away with it!" However, such was the persuasive skill of counsel, the outraged constable finally relented.

Unfortunately, it was not unusual in the Calgary of a gentler age to have the legitimacy of one's ancestry called upon in courts of law. It is said that Magistrate Gilbert Sanders, in questioning an ill-tempered Irishman accused of assault, asked why he was so quick to take offence. The accused replied, "Wouldn't you, if he had called *you* an Irish son-of-a-bitch?" Sanders calmly pointed out, in his proper British accent, that he wasn't Irish. At that the Irishman responded, "Well what if he called you the kind of son-of-a-bitch you *are?*"*

Magistrate Sanders was a very fine character who, despite his accent, was born and educated in British Columbia. He served in various wars, including the Boer War, held a commission in the Royal Canadian Mounted Police, and ended his career as a police magistrate in Calgary. He was said to have been more British than the English. He wore a monocle, even in his sleep, and was every inch the professional soldier, but he was filled with the milk of human kindness.

He was a striking figure on the bench. His worldly experience was so great that he seemed to sense guilt or innocence, but sometimes he convicted on evidence which the Appellate Division of the Supreme Court of Alberta held to be insufficient to establish guilt beyond any reasonable doubt, and they would quash his conviction. Completely unrepentant and undaunted, the Colonel would denounce their Lordships' decision in his own open court.

Following the disastrous market crash in the fall of 1929, the Attorney General of Alberta and his counterpart in Ontario embarked upon a series of prosecutions of stock brokers for various and sundry offences against the Criminal Code of Canada. One of these brokers was a highly respected Calgarian named Clive Betts whose firm became bankrupt. Fortunately he was able to secure another position in the brewing business in Ontario but he was charged, arrested, brought back to Calgary, pleaded not guilty and was given a preliminary hearing before Colonel Sanders. A special prosecutor from the Attorney General's Department in Edmonton appeared for the Crown and informed the Magistrate that the Premier wished the accused to be committed for trial without fail. The Colonel had a fine sense of justice and fair play. Said he to the special prosecutor, "Tell the Premier I will commit the accused if, and *only* if, there is sufficient evidence to put him on trial!" The hearing proceeded and His Worship dismissed the charges for lack of sufficient evidence.

He was fired by the Attorney General the same day.

Colonel Sanders, although never a student of the law, had long been a highly respected and popular citizen in his various capacities as soldier, police officer and magistrate. The Calgary Bar attended a luncheon in his honour which was filled to overflowing. No mention was made of the Betts Case or his dismissal, but those present gave the Colonel a series of standing ovations.

Facing Page: *Magistrate Gilbert Sanders was born in British Columbia but was said to have been more British than the English. He wore a monocle — even in his sleep — and was every inch the professional soldier.*

*Editor's note: This paragraph was written by the Editor from previously supplied information.

Progress at the Loyal Bank

by Anele Jenkins

Anele J. Jenkins was born in Lithuania and came to Canada as a youngster where her family took up residence in Langdon, Alberta. Anele received her education primarily in Calgary and Edmonton and emerged finally as a school teacher.

During the Second World War and prior to her marriage to Ronald Jenkins (of the Jenkins Groceteria chain), "Nell" held various administrative positions with medical, legal and oil business firms. She was a charter member of the Doctor George Kerby chapter of the IODE, a member of the Calgary Sketch Club, the Business and Professional Women's Club, and the Calgary Press Club among many others.

As I sit here and reminisce
Do you know what I really miss?
That small stone building, dark and dank
That used to be the Loyal Bank.

As I look back in retrospect
The bank was held in great respect.
And to "deposit", or "withdraw"
You entered it in greatest awe.

The manager, as I recall,
A well-known figure to us all,
Wore tailored suit and diamond pin
And greeted you as you came in.

The teller in his wire cage
Was male, of somewhat younger age,
And tho' he wore an elbow patch
Was eyed by gals as quite a catch.

The Junior, and, — God bless the lad,
Showed promise (or so thought his dad).
The bank's the place for such as he,
Someday, a banker he will be!

And then the steno, neat and trim,
The only person not a "him",
Was object of each silly prank
Being a female in a bank.

They all knew just how much you had,
And if your loan was good or bad.
They knew that when you couldn't pay,
You crossed the street the other way.

Now that was fifty years ago
And I have seen and watched it grow.
It is no longer dark and dank,
That skyscraper, the Loyal Bank.

The Junior, who would banker be,
Is now the manager we don't see.
A long, long way he really came –
Except that clerks don't know his name!

And, like the victims of some hex,
The tellers had a change of sex,
And now that female forms prevail
They *need* that cage for any male!

And even errors aren't the same
For you have no one you can blame.
And tho' they're sometimes caught in lies
Computers don't apologize!

They add, subtract and change amounts
Compute the interest on accounts,
And give the customer his share
But have no heart to really care.

Just fifty years have done all this
And, if my guess I do not miss,
Another fifty years will bring
A change in this computer thing.

A talking robot will replace
Each human hand and smiling face.
Star Wars' creator we will thank
For Space Staff in the Loyal Bank!

The Imperial Bank of Canada joined the festivities by draping the building in colourful bunting to celebrate Calgary's first Stampede in September of 1912.

Below: *The Bank of Montreal on the northeast corner of Eighth Avenue and First Street West was at the hub of downtown Calgary in the late '20s.*

FIRST BAPTIST CHURCH
CALGARY

The Minister's Cat

by Marguerite Langille

Marguerite (McLellan) Langille arrived in Calgary in 1912 with her parents. She was educated in the city schools and at the University of Alberta where she obtained her teaching certificate. After marrying E.G. Langille, a mining engineer, she and her husband were stationed at the Premier Gold Mine near Stewart, British Columbia. The next thirteen years were spent in the gold mining towns of B.C. until 1953 when the family returned to Calgary to take up permanent residence once more. Mrs. Langille still attends the First Baptist Church but the David Lloyd George of her story has, no doubt, moved on.

In the days before radio and television there wasn't much for respectable young Calgarians to do on Sunday evenings except attend church. Fortunately for us, Dr. H.H. Bingham, who preached at First Baptist in the 1920s, was a dynamic speaker who engaged and entertained us youngsters with the down-to-earth practicality of his sermons. Not much could discompose him — as we learned to our amusement one evening in early spring.

First Baptist and the manse next door were home to David Lloyd George, the Bingham's huge Persian cat. Like his namesake, this great, white-maned tabby was an animal of no half measure. He was clever, tending to be ruthless in fact, and he had an uncanny ability to persuade most human adversaries to follow his lead.

Now this particular spring Sunday afternoon a happy young couple was married at the church. David Lloyd George — no sentamentalist he — bored by the foofaraw, jumped into the back seat of the newlyweds' car for a nap in the warm sun.

Following the ceremony the couple was ushered into the honeymoon car by the wedding attendants with cheerful good-byes to hurry them along on their wedding trip to Banff. David Lloyd George was no doubt annoyed by the interruption in his snooze, but he settled back down to enjoy his rest, gently rocked by the moving car.

It wasn't until the rough country road rudely jarred him awake that David Lloyd George peckishly announced his presence. Surprised, the honeymooners turned around to find the source of the commotion and resigned themselves to the trip all the way back to the manse — no small undertaking in those days.

Dr. H.H. Bingham surrounded by members of the First Baptist Church Sunday School class in the 1920s.

By the time David Lloyd George was delivered home and dropped with a resentful thump on the Church steps, the evening service was well under way. With a swish of his imperious tail to bid the newlyweds farewell, the cat sauntered into the church and down the centre aisle.

Those of us high in the top gallery of the sanctuary had a bird's-eye view of Dr. Bingham preaching a heartfelt final admonition, unaware of the comic relief slowly wending his way toward the pulpit. Naturally, the younger the audience the funnier was the response to the sight, and those of us who were teenagers were convulsed with ill-suppressed hysteria by the time Dr. Bingham realized the reason for the uproar.

He looked down as David Lloyd George wound his ample tail around his ankles, paused only a moment to pass the cat to the organist and finished his sermon with a flourish. It was hard to decide just whose composure remained most unruffled, Dr. Bingham's or David Lloyd George's! Truly they were a pair well suited for one another's company.

Ghost Horse

by Robert Standish

Robert H. Standish was born just south of Calgary and following high school attended the Calgary Normal School. He taught school in Okotoks and built a teacherage in Fordsville where, by the early 1940s he had reached the one hundred dollar a month pinnacle of teacher pay. Such good fortune he could hardly afford, so in 1941 Mr. Standish retired to go into the oil business, where he remained for the next thirty years.

I think of myself as a native Calgarian, although I suppose technically that's not true.

My grandfather and grandmother, with their four boys all under nine years old, arrived in the North-West Territories from Ontario in March, 1886 and homesteaded near the present corner of Blackfoot Trail and Heritage Drive. Grandfather thought Calgary was "too crowded", so he moved to Innisfail where, again being overcrowded, they obtained a homestead in the Priddis area in 1891. I was born there and received my elementary education nearby. By 1923 I was ready to re-establish a family footprint on Calgary's domain and spent three years at Central Collegiate Institute, (better known in those days as the Calgary Collection of Idiots). It was during those commuter days that I had my encounter with the Ghost Horse.

As soon as classes ended on Fridays I would set out for home on foot, about twenty-six miles as the crow flies, over the Weaselhead Bridge on the Elbow River, across the Sarcee Indian Reserve to home, arriving in about six hours. My sister was smarter than I; she hired a horse from Ruttle's Stable and rode home, but I couldn't be bothered to wait for a horse regardless of the fact that she arrived first!

One dark night in the autumn before the leaves had fallen, I was racing across the Sarcee Reserve when a snow-white horse stepped out of a clump of willows in front of me. With an abrupt surge of adrenalin, I raced faster than any four-legged animal could have, and that night I was home before my sister!

I often wondered if my parents ever knew why I was anxious, all of a sudden, to be driven back to Calgary in the buggy. The weekend walks through the countryside were never again quite so leisurely.

In Praise of
My Foster Father

by Janet Mitchell

Janet Mitchell was born in Medicine Hat in 1915. As an infant, Miss Mitchell was reared by foster parents in Calgary. Upon the death of her mother, however, she was left in the care of her father, who raised her as best he could using what homemaking skills he could remember or invent. Miss Mitchell's memories of those times are as poignant as they are colourful.

Although she had no artistic background and only little exposure to art in school, she "grew into" her art as she matured. In 1942 Miss Mitchell won a scholarship to the Banff School of Fine Arts and then took evening classes under the direction of Illingworth Kerr. For many years she worked as an income tax assessor and painted only as a hobby, but as her artistic reputation spread she was able to retire in 1963 to spend full time at her easel. Her works in oils and watercolours are widely represented across Canada, including landscapes at the Glenbow Museum, Calgary, and the National Gallery of Canada.

I was nine years old in 1924 when my foster mother died and John Mitchell and I were left alone to cope as best we could in our little house in Sunnyside. For the next three years he was more than my guardian; he was my protector and teacher, and I look back with gratitude at that good man.

I suppose that in today's society no small girl would be allowed to continue living in such circumstances with such a foster father. His language was atrocious, but, being a widower, he was probably unaccustomed to blushing female ears. It wasn't unusual for him to react to my misdemeanours with a ringing, "I'm going to break your bloody neck!" But that was as far as his punishments ever got — the threat kept me in line and he never needed to let down the tough Scot's image he liked to project.

On Wednesday nights he would take my hand for our walk down to the Armouries, where he was a Quarter Master Sergeant with the Tenth Batallion Calgary Highlanders. He would

*John Mitchell was a Quarter Master Sergeant of the Tenth Battalion
Calgary Highlanders. On parade nights, the proud swagger of his kilt
celebrated his Scottish ancestry.*

never have left me alone, and I suspect that he enjoyed having me along on those parade nights. While I perched high on the balcony above the parade square listening to the band music, the manoeuvres went on below and I could see the proud swagger of his kilt. Later I was bedded down between two chairs in the storeroom but I could overhear the laughter of the men telling their racy stories — stories that were far beyond the understanding of a small girl.

At the end of the evening, he woke me for our walk home up Tenth Street North, across the Louise Bridge, and, in the fall of the year, we always stopped at the city garden plots so that he could help himself to an ingredient or two for his ever-ever soup pot. Those vegetables, with a generous measure of barley, bubbled away in the Scotch broth which he bragged was "so thick you can dance on it!" It, together with the strong black tea and occasional treat of fish and chips, was my diet for as long as I lived with John Mitchell. To this day I get queasy remembering those meals.

Dad worked night duty at the CPR station and often, if I wasn't already asleep, I would be invited to come along. A shelf in the baggage room would become my bed and a mail bag my pillow, and I happily dozed off listening to the conversations of the men at work with the rumbling of the trains to lull me to sleep.

It's true that no social worker today could look at such a man — teeth blackened from tobacco, and profanity spilling over every sentence — and see a fit candidate to father a small girl. But I was happy with John Mitchell. He gave generously of his time, and his gruffness was never able to quite hide the affection in which he held me. I loved him.

Home Ties

by Alison Jackson

Alison M. Jackson was born in Calgary and received her elementary and high school education in this city. After graduating from the University of Alberta with her BA degree, Alison started to work at the Calgary Public Library. Here she worked for thirty-eight years, taking time off to secure a Bachelor's degree in librarianship from the University of Washington in Seattle and a Master's degree in library science from the University of Michigan. She worked chiefly in the Cataloguing Department, and was in charge of this department for seventeen years.

Of her parents Miss Jackson writes: "My father, Gavin Miller Jackson, was born in Scotland in 1878. Recovering from a ruptured lung, he came to western Canada in 1904 with the hope of regaining his health in this climate. He was followed a short time later by his brother William, and for almost two years they worked on a farm near Airdrie. Then, in 1906, they left the farm to settle in Calgary where they established the Jackson Bakery on Fifteenth Avenue, Southwest. Later my father went into business as a partner and manager of the Model Bakery in Hillhurst. He died in 1953.

My mother, Gertrude (Lewis) Jackson, was born in Toronto in 1878 of an English family which had settled there in the 1840s. Mother came to Calgary in 1909, accompanying a married sister. She fell in love with the young western city, and never to the end of her long life wanted to leave Calgary, either to visit her old home or to travel. Mother died in 1975 at the age of ninety-six."

In 1924 my father planned a trip back to Scotland to show his young Canadian family — my mother, my sister and me — to his folks at home. The years had slipped by while he had been building up a bakery business in the small and growing city of Calgary, and this was his first trip home in twenty years.

My mother, a stay-at-home person, very reluctantly left her home, garden, and all the familiar associations in Calgary, and most unwillingly set out on the long train trip across Canada to Montreal, followed by the dreaded week-long voyage to Glasgow.

After visiting among relatives in the little Scottish village, Father decided that a trip down to southern England and the city of London would be interesting and enjoyable. The British Empire Exhibition at Wembley was in full swing that summer, and Father planned to take us there

Colonel James Walker's tall and commanding figure was familiar to every Calgarian. In 1975 he was bestowed with the prestigious and deserved title: "Citizen of the Century".

to see the sights. For him the Canada Building was a principal attraction, and I can recall the huge sculpture in butter, and the glasses of fruit from Canadian orchards.

While studying with interest many of the exhibits, Father happened to glance up as a familiar tall and commanding figure entered the room. "Why there's Colonel Walker!" exclaimed my father in delighted tones, as Colonel James Walker, the North-West Mounted Police pioneer of early Calgary, approached. Suddenly, breaking away from Father, my mother darted forward and ran up to the Colonel, flung her arms around the astonished gentleman, and cried out, "Oh Calgary, Calgary!" Father, embarrassed and flustered, hurried after her, but Colonel Walker smiled reassuringly and said, "It's all right, Jackson. She's just homesick for Calgary."

Only recently I was reminded of my childhood trip to Scotland when I discovered part of my father's memoirs tucked away in a box of keepsakes. Reading the excerpt brought back a flash of memory because I, as a twelve year old child, stood with him to witness that beautiful sunset on Lake Superior. It happened that we were on our way to his native country, but such was his love for his adopted home that he wrote this moving testament to its beauty.

An Image, A Memory

by Gavin M. Jackson

How often it happens that, in looking for wonders afar off, we overlook greater marvels at our very door. Who is there who has visited or lived in Calgary in October and failed to notice our wondrous sunsets? Sunsets that no human artist may ever do justice to with either tongue or pen or brush. I once saw a sunset on Lake Superior and that sight is, I believe, world-famous and justly so. The sun sinking like a great ball of fire in a landless horizon, and its reflection, an enormous tongue of fire reaching along the lake's surface to swallow the ship. A marvel of creation, the most marvelous I had ever seen, and yet, last week, just ten miles from my own home, I saw another even more wonderful.

I was motoring westward from Strathmore toward Calgary; the sun was just dipping behind the Rockies, and the western sky was a blazing expanse of red gold, with the jagged line of the Rockies showing black below. Driving was extremely difficult, the blinding brilliance above making it almost impossible to see the road. I had just remarked to my companion that we'd have to look out for the bend around Chestermere Lake or I might drive into the water, when suddenly, the lake burst into view, a complete replica, inverted, of the brilliance above. One had to stop and gape in sheer amazement. A perfect reflection of the red-gold sky mirrored in the water, and, above it, the jagged line and black mass of the Rockies hanging upside down. No human artist could possibly paint that and do it a tithe of justice; if he could and did, his canvas would be labelled a "gross exaggeration".

Prairie Blizzard

by Margaret Howard

Margaret (Hannah) Howard was born in Calgary in 1920, the daughter of George and Mary Hannah, and was raised in the northeast area of the city. Her father, G.A. Hannah, was a pioneer of early Calgary and was the founding partner of Riverside Ironworks.

After graduating from the University of Alberta, Margaret interned at the Sick Children's Hospital in Toronto and began her career as a hospital dietician at the Holy Cross and Colonel Belcher Hospitals in Calgary. She was married in 1950 and became a full time homemaker and mother to the family's three children, but she has retained the memories of her own childhood and recalls them here to share with others of her generation.

As a little girl during the late 1920s and 1930s, I attended Stanley Jones School which stood solidly in sandstone majesty against the prairie elements in northeast Calgary. Even in my day there had not been much development; the municipal airport was north of the school and the old Regal Golf Course was farther out, but still to the east across the flat could be seen a scattering of farmhouses.

Each spring the field surrounding the school was covered with purple crocuses, and in the grassy margins meadowlarks nested with their spotted eggs. In winter though, deep snow covered the ground and we were dressed for our long trek to school in woolen underwear with leggings and sweaters, muffled in toques with our scarves wound about our faces. With our leather moccasins laced high over our ankles, we would run and slide our way to school on crisp days that sparkled with hoar frost.

One winter afternoon, when I was about seven years old, we perched high in our wooden desks watching the sky outside threaten with dark, gusting clouds that whipped toward us from the north. By late afternoon the temperature had dropped alarmingly and the blizzard's freezing winds built high irregular snow drifts. We could no longer see across the field toward the safety of our homes. Our teachers were frightened to send us into the storm, so it was decided that the old school would be our best shelter.

I'm sure that our excitement was fueled by that undercurrent of fear, but we clustered

We struggled over drifts and were slid across the ice by the howling winds until finally we saw the welcoming lights of home.

about the windows peering through the swirling snow until we made out a figure bent against the wind making his way across that open field. As he approached, I could see my father's familiar cap pulled down low over his ears to meet the plaid muffler covering his face, so that only frosty eyebrows and lashes were visible. Over his shoulder he had looped a strong rope. Our rescuer had arrived.

There was much awe in our wide-eyed silence as my cousins and I were wrapped tightly in our scarves, and bound around the waist by Father's long rope at intervals of about three feet. At last we began our long trip home. Father leading, and my biggest cousin tied in last place along the rope, we struggled over drifts and were slid across the ice by the howling winds until finally we saw the welcoming lights of home.

Hot thick soup and homemade brown bread awaited our arrival. That evening must have been an anxious one for our parents, but, for those of us who were children, it was a day of high adventure, and remains a vivid memory of growing up in Calgary.

From the very beginning, the Parade was a highlight of Stampede Week, and spectators, bedecked in bowlers and straw boaters, sought viewpoints atop bunting-draped office buildings.

Stampede Shirts

by Gladys Johnson

Gladys (Dunlop) Johnson speaks with great enthusiasm about her involvement with The Native Calgarian Society, and with justifiable awe about the circumstances of her arrival in the pioneer city. She was born in 1914, by Caesarian section, on a kitchen table in Upper Hillhurst. Following high school, Gladys worked as a clerk at Eaton's until her marriage in 1937. The next four years were spent in British Columbia. In 1941 however, the family returned to Calgary where her three children were raised and, after Mrs. Johnson retired from her career in motherhood, she became assistant buyer and staff supervisor at the Tall Shops. She now volunteers her free hours at the Glenbow Museum, Calgary.

Mrs. Johnson's mother was a shirtmaker whose skills were much sought after by the early citizens of Calgary. "In the early days," Mrs. Johnson writes, "shirts were really well made, with flat fell seams and two pieces in the sleeve. Many were made from pure silk purchased by Mother's customers while on trips to India or China, and for those special orders Mom charged a dollar and twenty-five cents to cut and make a shirt."

By the early 1920s Calgary was recovering from the effects of the First World War and the 1918 Flu, and the Stampede was really coming into its own. My mother, who by trade made gentlemen's shirts, had an offer from the Hudson's Bay store to make several dozen by early June. It seems there had been requests from ranchers who wanted matching shirts for their riders to wear in the upcoming rodeo. Mom felt she could meet this challenge, so she bought a Hamilton Beach motor for her faithful Singer and a buttonhole machine. We lived in a big old-fashioned house with the living room and dining room separated by an archway, so it was easy to push things aside to set up shop.

Good quality cotton sateen in bright colours was chosen: sunshine yellow, deep orange, royal purple, cerise, and emerald green. The next step was to transfer the patterns to strong brown paper. Bolts of materials arrived with thread and buttons, and the job was underway. Mom and Dad cut the fabrics in the evening, and the next day the machine would hum. After school I'd clip threads or sew on buttons and then the finished product was pressed on the kitchen table. (Who ever heard of an ironing board?) When the job was completed it was a real thrill to watch

Stampede Parade.
Calgary 1924

In the early '20s, the ranchers ordered custom-made matching shirts for their cowboys riding in the Stampede Parade.

the parade and see the cowboys attired in shirts that we had made in our dining room.

I guess the project was a success because the next year the Bay came to Mom much earlier. She rented three machines and hired four girls, so one was free to sew on buttons, press and fold, while the others did the stitching. The name "emerald green" was changed to "seasick green" since one of the girls became quite ill any time she tried to work with the green fabric.

One family of ropers and riders ordered shirts made of Connaught satin, in lovely cornflower blue and white. I remember it well because the boys wanted their initials embroidered on the pockets and it was my job to do the monogramming. All was going well until Mom noticed I had turned the "J" backwards. No harm was done; Mom made another pocket and I finally got it right. It still amuses me because, since I married a Johnson, believe me, I now know which way to turn a "J"!

Mom made the Stampede shirts for several years, but, as the interest in Western dress grew, the orders were given to factories in the East, so an era ended for us. We all agreed though, that while we worked hard, we had fun and met a great many interesting people.

128

How Many Please?

by Grace Shaw

She was a little lady — just over five feet tall — but she ran the box office at The Grand Theatre with stature and style. Annie Wilson accepted the job in 1915. When she first sat down behind the wicket, she couldn't reach over the counter to pass out the tickets, so the manager had a platform built that served a dual purpose. It made her tall enough to do the job and it held the cradle occupied by her baby daughter. While Mrs. Wilson's foot rocked the cradle, she was filling the house. "How many please?"

Nobody called this genial lady, Annie. She was Mrs. Wilson. Her domain was the front of the house and her job was to fill every seat. As treasurer of the theatre, she negotiated prices with the advance agents of the road shows. Sir Harry Lauder's agent tried to dicker with her over the price of admission tickets but even though he got the act, she set the prices. She knew the city and how much local patrons would pay.

When a show came to Calgary called, "It Pays to Advertise", the manager was out of town, so Mrs. Wilson decided to get into the advertising business. She persuaded the city electrical department to string coloured lights from the corner of First Street and Eighth Avenue right up to the entrance of the Grand Theatre. The novelty brought in the people, and the manager approved. She put a display of shoes in the lobby, and Union Milk advertised with a huge milk bottle. Even with all of these promotions she never forgot her own salespitch: "How many please?"

On one occasion extensive promotional material was mailed to the businessmen of Calgary reading "Call this number now. A young lady would like to speak to you." The box office phone rang constantly, and the tickets were selling rapidly, but one caller was anything but receptive. When Mrs. Wilson answered, a woman's angry voice snapped, "There's a young lady there that wants to speak to my husband. I'm his wife and *I'll* take the message."

Mrs. Wilson had her regular patrons. She reserved a special box for Lady Lougheed and her daughter. Sir James came when he was not in Ottawa attending to his political duties, and, long before oil gushed in Turner Valley, R.A. Brown reserved a front box for all the vaudeville shows. Ranchmen's Club members sat in the front row every Monday night but their tickets were saved only until six-thirty. One gentleman arrived at the box office at eight-fifteen to find that his ticket had been sold. His irate response to this turn of events was too much for Mrs. Wilson. She got off her stool, stormed into the lobby with clenched fists, and, looking up at the tall man, she retorted: "Now, say that again to *this* lady!" The next day the biggest box of chocolates available in Calgary was delivered to her, "With apologies from Mr. Adams."

I Remember Duck Catching

by J.V.H. Milvain

James Valentine Hogarth Milvain, QC, LLD, was born, like his namesake, on February 14. His family ranched in southern Alberta but, since his birth occurred the year before the incorporation of the province, Mr. Milvain enjoys boasting of his birthplace as the North-West Territories.

During his early legal career he practised with J. Fred Scott, Hugh John MacDonald and W.K. Moore among others. In 1955 Mr. Milvain became a member of the Chambers Might law firm and, as chief counsel with H.J. Laycraft, argued and won the last Canadian case that went to the Judicial Committee of the Privy Council in London. Later in 1959, he was appointed to the Trial Division of the Supreme Court of Alberta, becoming its Chief Justice in 1968.

Following his retirement, Mr. Milvain was awarded an Honorary Doctorate of Laws by the University of Calgary and a city school was named in his honour. By way of relaxation he now likes to visit the old ranch in southern Alberta where, as a boy, he fished at Camp Creek and rode the grub line as a cowpuncher.

It was a beautiful sunny Saturday towards the end of May, 1927, but during the previous week there had been heavy rainfalls in Calgary. This made for clear pools of warm water in the grass-bottomed low-lying areas which formed wonderful playgrounds for many families of happy young ducks.

The Calgary Zoo was fairly new in those days, and a young lawyer by the name of J. Fred Scott, a zoo director, embarked upon a plan designed to capture a few ducklings for the watery areas of the park. He decided to organize duck-catching teams: three one-man teams armed with fishing nets and water gear, tempered with ample good humour, would venture out to the rolling

The woodland setting of St. George's Island could be enjoyed by early Calgarians on this footpath by the Bow River.

131

fields east of the city. There, he knew, would be many pools of clear rain water and dozens of young ducks.

We were an easy lot to recruit. I was Scott's newly articled law student and, since it was customary in those days for lawyers to work on Saturday mornings, a free day off in the warm spring air was an offer too good to refuse. Scott's pal Eric Harvie, another young lawyer and polo teammate, joined us for the adventure, and we headed out to the country.

The day was an enormous success from all points of view. Our catch happily lived on at the zoo producing the countless generations that have profited by their change of habitat, and we three had the time of our lives.

I doubt that our spring-fever-induced day away from work did us much harm. Fred Scott became the commanding officer of the Calgary Highlanders at the outbreak of the Second World War and is remembered and honoured for his services to his community by the school named after him in northeast Calgary. Eric Harvie, of course, later became a millionaire oilman and philanthropist, and that young student eventually went along in the law to become Chief Justice of the Trial Division of the Supreme Court of Alberta.

St. George's Island
Calgary No. 71

Facing Page: *The entry to St. George's Island in the twenties was a splendid lamplit avenue.*

Below: *St. George's Island 1912. This building, known as the "Biergarten", was a predecessor of the present Aviary tea room.*

Frank's cousin's house was about a third of the way down the block, but he could turn into their gate every time without having to ask anyone for directions. His nine-year-old audience was fascinated! Did he count the number of steps from the corner, or was it just his uncanny sense of direction?

'Blind Mac' Macdonald

by Carl Cummer

Carl Cummer was born in 1903 in Ontario and came west to Calgary in 1910. He attended Connaught School but when he was fourteen he injured his back severely and spent the next three years confined to bed.

Following his convalescence, he enrolled in Garbutt's Business College. In 1925 he became an employee of the City Clerk's office and worked thirty-seven years with that department, retiring in 1963.

No collection of stories about Calgarians during the early part of the century would be complete without one about Frank Macdonald. He was referred to as "Blind Mac" and most of his friends called him "Mac" rather than Frank.

Mac was blind from the date of his birth. I met him often when he visited his cousin who lived across the street from us on Thirteenth Avenue Southwest. I was about nine or ten years old in 1912 and I recall being impressed by Frank's ability to walk along the street by tapping his white cane on the concrete sidewalk ahead of him for guidance. As kids do, some of us would test our own ability to do the same by blindfolding ourselves and trying to find our way to the end of the block without veering off the sidewalk. His cousin's house was about a third of the way down the block, but he could turn into their gate every time without having to ask anyone for directions. Did he count the number of steps from the corner or was it just his uncanny sense of direction?

It wasn't until many years later when I worked in the City Clerk's office at City Hall, that I came to know Frank really well. The CNIB had set up a concession stand across the hallway from our office and Frank was put in charge. The shop carried numerous brands of candies, chocolate bars and cigarettes, as well as a few other odds and ends, but it wasn't long before he knew where to put his hands on anything that was asked for. It also wasn't long before he was calling everyone by name, since he was able to identify the sounds of voices.

I walked uptown with Frank many times. He would take my arm lightly and let me lead about a step ahead of him. That way he could keep pace no matter how fast I stepped out. It wasn't necessary to slow down for curbs either, since he could sense from the motion of my body when to step down or up to another level.

Frank boarded with Jock Bailey who worked at the Post Office. The Baileys had eight children and Frank was like a member of the family to them all. If Frank was out for an evening, Jock would never retire until he was safely home again. The Baileys lived west of Second Street East on Thirteenth Avenue, which was handy for Frank since it was just a short distance to the Belt Line streetcar. And, since he had honed his highly developed sense of hearing to the point that he was able to moonlight as a professional piano tuner, he used the transit system frequently.

It was, as a matter of fact, a badly tuned piano that began our close friendship.

A few years after my wife and I were married, we rented a house in Sunnyside and an old Heintzman piano went along with the place. I couldn't play but, having taken violin lessons, I had a good ear for music and could tell it was badly in need of tuning. I asked Frank to take on the job.

It was a revelation to see him go about it. I looked in when he opened the top and couldn't see any sign of a screw because of all the dust and lint, but in no time at all, with the aid of his sensitive fingers, Frank located every screw that had to be removed before he could take off the front of the piano. I told him how dirty it was, so he said he had better take the keys off so I could clean under the mechanism as well. With that he took off more parts, then ran his arm under the lower batch of keys and, holding his other arm over them, placed the keys on the piano bench. He did this two or three times more so that I could then do the vacuuming. His fingers ran over the leather buckles that needed replacing and he did that repair without difficulty and assured me that the felts on the hammers were intact and showed no sign of moth damage.

It wasn't long until the piano was in tune. When it was all put back together, Mac sat down and played for us. As he played I took my violin from its case and joined in. I had never mentioned to him that I played the violin so he was surprised that I could play by ear as he did. But I could never pick up a tune as fast as Frank was able to; he could hear a new piece on the radio a time or two and master it right away in every key.

From that time on, Mac and I were bosom pals. Many Sundays we'd invite him for supper. He used to say that my wife was the best cook in town. After supper we would spend hours together making music for our own enjoyment. We seemed to unconsciously anticipate what the other was planning and at times he would switch to harmony while I carried the melody, and vice versa.

Mac loved to play for dances. He could always round up three or four other musicians when he had an engagement to play, but he never had a steady orchestra of his own. He managed to get by on what he made from his piano tuning and the CNIB concession stand.

I used to lead him around our garden in the summertime and tell him about the various plants growing there, and would have him feel the foliage of the developing vegetables. That was something that no one had thought of doing before. It was surprising to me that he hadn't known that corn grew on tall stalks. Mac could read braille as fast as I could read printing but I suppose I don't recall ever having *read* that corn grew on stalks. I think the greater part of our knowledge must be acquired visually. Whoever said "A picture is worth a thousand words" was so right. To have missed the little things that are commonplace to the sighted, like beautiful butterflies and colourful birds, whose loveliness words alone cannot describe, is something that could never be compensated for.

Mac Macdonald has been gone for many years now. St. Mary's Cathedral was filled with friends at the occasion of his funeral. I'm sure they all felt as fortunate as I that Mac had allowed us to see the beauty that lay beyond sight.

A Personal Account

by Ben Halbert

Benjamin Gold Halbert arrived in Calgary enroute to Trochu Valley in April, 1912. He was in Calgary before the first Stampede, before gas arrived from Bow Island and before the railway arrived in Trochu. A former coal miner, school principal and Second World War army sergeant, he is a forty-year member of the Canadian Legion, *an active member of the Southwood United Church, a visiting resource volunteer to Calgary Public and Separate Schools and president of the Southwood Seniors' Club. Now retired, Ben and his wife Grace share an active life and many pleasant memories of pioneer Alberta.*

Though my family arrived in Alberta in April of 1912, we might not have made it at all!

As part of that great wave of four hundred thousand European emigrants answering the call of the CPR, the Halberts booked passage on the Titanic bound for the new world. Fortunately our reservations were cancelled to make way for more affluent passengers and we set sail instead on the S.S. Saturnic. I was less than four years old at the time but I do remember the ten days we spent on the colonist train that meandered its way across Canada to our final destination in Calgary. We arrived just before Guy Weadick's first Stampede, and Father began making plans to homestead in the Trochu Valley.

Although my early years were spent in rural Alberta, I returned to the city in 1928 to attend the Calgary Normal School. Fortunately I was able to find a place to board on Seventeenth Avenue Northwest where, for thirty dollars a month, I was housed and fed. Since everything north of the house was bald prairie, for sport in the evenings we shot our limit of gophers. Each Friday evening my roommate and I ran down to the old YMCA on Ninth Avenue between Centre and First Streets East to take boxing lessons from Alex Wilson. I hasten to add that our pace back home was considerably slower.

The year 1928 was an exciting one for me in many ways. I went for my first airplane ride with Scotty McCall who used a field west of Calgary for a runway and took sightseeing passengers for flips through the skies of the foothills in his open-to-the-wind two-seater. That same year my roommate and I built a crystal radio in our room. Using the bed spring for an aerial and the radiator as a ground, we were able to pick up both radio stations.

The next year, however, plunged all of Alberta into the hard times of the Depression. It's strange, but now I'm more likely to remember the good times that we salvaged from the era — times like Sunday afternoons at the Crystal Swimming Pool or the summertime street car rides to Bowness Park. Those were the days that my spare nickel could buy a good cigar or a stamp to mail a letter to my girlfriend, or an ice cream cone or a slice of pie.

At the outbreak of the Second World War, I joined many of my fellow teachers in answering the call to duty, and was assigned to headquarters staff of the Royal Canadian Medical Corps in Calgary. This meant that I had to move into town from the small eastern Alberta community where I had been teaching, so, since real estate was still cheap and housing was at a premium, I decided to buy a house. For just over one thousand dollars, at fifty dollars a month interest-free, I purchased a house from the city at 421 Tenth Avenue Southeast, (which I was able to sell after the war for twelve thousand five hundred dollars!)

At District Medical Stores we received alcohol shipped to us in forty-five gallon drums. Of course those were the years of strict rationing and liquor was among the commodities most hoarded. Many non-coms "donated" their liquor permits to buy liquid refreshments for the officers' parties, so most of us quickly learned how to make the most of our favoured position in the medical stores. It was our job to transfer the pure, colourless alcohol from the forty-five gallon drums to smaller bottles. Usually there would be a surplus of about three-quarters of a gallon to each drum,

In spite of wartime rationing, the home front was a pretty exciting place to be back in 1941. At the Legion you could get a five cent glass of beer, a dollar haircut and a cheap lunch. And at night, there were always the dances!

and I'm sorry to say that often that surplus never reached the stockroom.

One day, however, an urgent telegram reached us at Medical Stores saying that, due to an oversight, the red dye that was supposed to be mixed with the wood alcohol (to distinguish it from the pure variety) had been left out of a shipment. You can imagine our reaction!

We never quite trusted the suppliers after that, and turned instead to the soldiers' hangouts in downtown Calgary: the theatres, Bucket of Blood Dance Halls, and the Southern Chicken Inn. The Legion was home to the serviceman in those days. It was there he could get a five cent glass of beer, a dollar haircut and a cheap lunch, all in time for an afternoon of poker where the limit was twenty-five cents with a maximum of three bumps.

Eventually we realized that the war would drag on without much regard for our family's convenience, so it was decided that my wife and sons would join me in Calgary. They arrived in 1942. While the boys attended Christopher Robin School, my wife taught at Montessori School and established a firm base on which to begin our post-war life together. So, when I was discharged in 1945, I continued my career in education, first as a social studies teacher, then as a high school principal.

It's unlikely that any of us in that great immigration wave of 1912 could have foreseen the upheavals that awaited us in our new homeland, but neither could we have predicted the bounty that has been ours beyond measure.

Sandstone Classics

by Bob Wallace

Bob Wallace was born in the community of Springbank in 1906. He attended Central Collegiate Institute in Calgary for the final year of high school and then enrolled in the Normal School for his teacher training. It was following these years that Mr. Wallace began teaching, but such was his dedication to his career that he continued his education during summer sessions at the University of Alberta. Fortunately for his young students, Mr. Wallace's life-long interest in track and field made him an active booster of his schools' teams.

I was a young teacher in 1928, with only two years experience in rural one-room schools, when I was posted to Riverside Elementary School. It was one of Calgary's classic eight-room sandstone schools, and already outdated, but it was home to me for the next seventeen years. Through the years I was to witness the school's evolution to junior high status and would succeed Mr. J.W. Verge as principal, but most of my lingering nightmares have to do with the school's physical deterioration. We managed to overcome the obstacles presented by the demands of the rapidly modernizing curriculum, but it was a game that had to be played for the love of the sport — not because we ever thought we could win the contest.

By 1935, Riverside Elementary had become Langevin Junior High School. Somehow a gymnasium would have to be found that would meet at least minimal requirements for physical education classes. There was no playground and the school's two basement playrooms had already been pressed into service for the shop and home economics classes. The only available space was on the top floor. To this day I close my eyes and cringe, remembering how I tried to teach while the ceiling above cracked and heaved as adolescent phys. ed. classes were put through their paces above our heads. Depression era budgets were sadly inadequate to meet our needs. It was pointless to ask that the plant be modernized when we knew that there was really no money to even keep abreast of repair work, but some guardian angel must have seen our pitiful state of affairs.

Election time rolled around as inevitable as death and taxes, and our auditorium was host to campaigning candidates. In the heat of battle our "angel" appeared in the guise of a robust lady seeking re-election to the school board, who, to emphasize her argument, stomped her foot right through the stage floor! Two days later repairmen arrived.

Riverside Elementary, as so many sandstone schools in Calgary, was notorious for its third floor gym. Second floor teachers, though, taught valiantly on while ceilings above cracked and heaved from the exertions of adolescent phys. ed. classes.

But patch work, we all knew, could never keep up with the demands put on our old school, and we played a constant game of make-do-or-do-without. It was with some measure of relief that I faced a change of schools in 1949.

I was transferred as principal to King Edward School — another sandstone school — but this one a great deal larger than old Langevin. Our twenty classrooms, however, were quickly filled and then brimmed over, with playrooms, shop and home ec. rooms put into service to house 850 students. At one point, in fact, our grade nines lived homeless with no home room to accommodate them. Fortunately our students treated their hardship as a point of pride and, despite the inadequate facilities, rose above the challenge and excelled.

At King Edward we were forced to use a wide main floor hallway for a gym and, because playground space was limited, South Calgary Park was pressed into service. Year after year, however, springtime brought renewed enthusiastic school spirit and triumph at city-wide track meets. I remember well the June day that a police escort marched beside our victorious track team supported on the shoulders of their student body. The parade wound all the way back to the school, heads held high, banners waving and pride beaming in every young smile. Greater odds had never been overcome.

I stayed at King Edward for seventeen years, and, like the children, learned to have a special pride in those sandstone schools. They were sadly outdated and overcrowded, yet I regret each time I hear that another has gone the way of the wrecker's ball.

These eleven year olds at King Edward School sit solemnly at attention, momentarily kept out of mischief. Like generations of Calgary school children, though, they no doubt left their marks on the old wrought iron and hardwood, flip-seated desks that lined up in rows as rigid as ramrods.

The Double Barrel Gun Club

by A.R. Smith

Arthur R. Smith, born and educated in Calgary, is one of the few Canadians to have served as a city alderman, a Member of a Provincial Legislature, a Member of the House of Commons, and as a delegate to the United Nations.

He has also encompassed a broad commercial spectrum in his business career having served in the petroleum industry, as an executive officer of a national advertising and public relations company, as a publication editor,

and as president of a Southeast Asian industrial development company. He is currently President of Lavalin Services and Chairman of the Board of Worldwide Energy Corporation.

Mr. Smith's father, A.L. Smith, also a Member of Parliament, was a highly re-garded defense counsel. Stories about his trial work have become legendary in the legal community and his reputation as a Calgary "character" is well deserved.

About forty miles northeast of Calgary lies the town of Irricana and just prior to entering the outskirts of the town on Highway 9, a winding gravel road leads to a large slough that was once the home of the Double Barrel Gun Club.

I remember this venerable sporting institution because, as a boy during the 1930s, I accompanied my family on many a hunting expedition, sharing the back seat of an old Nash touring car with two dogs, an assortment of shotguns and cases of shells that carried a sticker price of a dollar and forty-five cents per carton.

Situated in the middle of a Hutterite Colony, the three-mile-long lake and surrounding swathed grain fields attracted thousands of ducks and geese because the migration flyaway had not yet shifted to the Saskatchewan border.

The central focus of the club was an old plywood two-story shack with detached outdoor plumbing reverently referred to as "the lodge" and, while its amenities were few, it nonetheless accommodated the members with six double bunks and floor mattresses.

The membership of the Double Barrel Gun Club consisted of some of our best-remembered sportsmen whose careers formed an indelible part of Calgary's fabric in the Depression years, and well ahead of their time these men accepted their wives as equal, if not better, hunting companions. Shown here is Sara Smith and a friend, with the day's bag.

The membership consisted of some of our best remembered sportsmen whose careers formed an indelible part of Calgary's fabric in the Depression years. Names like Eric Harvie, Kink Roenisch, Dr. Bob O'Callaghan, John Southam, Berry Berryman, Bob Heard, Chester De La Vergne, Sir Dudley Ward and Percy Barton all claimed membership, and well ahead of their time these men accepted their wives as equal, if not better hunting companions.

I can recall the pre-shoot evening strategy meetings when my father, A.L.Smith, the Hunt Master, would assign members to gun positions with such colourful names as Slaughter Point. The tactical discussion that carried on under candlelight into the night for the morning shoot would have done justice to the orchestration that launched the assult on the Normandy beachhead.

The club was not without its rules. In fact the Double Barrel Gun Club name was a terse statement that pump guns were not welcome, as one very embarrassed guest learned upon his arrival at the lodge. Assessment for each member was forty dollars a year. These funds paid for the Hutterite lease rental as well as a minimal salary for the off-season caretaker, an Englishman by the name of Tom Harrison.

My most vivid memory of the hunt was as a restless youngster preparing the cavalcade for the dusty drive back to Calgary. It was my assignment to induce the exhausted dogs back into the cars, load the trunk with as many birds as it would carry and then fall asleep in the back seat, not realizing that I was witness to an era that has long since disappeared into history.

The Victoria Inch Spoof

by Jack Peach

It was not until some time after his death that I recognized the prankster side of my father, Reg Peach. It was an aspect of him that was hidden from me because we had had trouble sharing ourselves with one another during his lifetime.

After he was gone I discovered he had been an intense and erudite multi-lingual scholar of legend and myth. So, when a religious sect descended upon Calgary, armed with their own book of revelations, hopeful of saving the city's sin-stained soul, clearly it was an opportunity for a practical joke.

Father's beloved and close colleague was George Fordyce, a scotch-loving Aberdonian architect of considerable skill and humour. Coincidently, at the particular time the religious group appeared, Reg Peach and George Fordyce were working on a renovation project for the Victoria Hotel which was situated on the south side of Eighth Avenue between Centre and First Streets East.

In revamping the hotel's facade they discovered that beneath a bland contemporary stucco finish there was a fine example of some early stonemason's craft. Skillfully fashioned sandstone blocks formed a splendid pattern of wall, sill, lintel and arch.

Meanwhile, the religious sect was peddling to anyone who would listen their theory that they were descended from the tribe chosen by God to lead the world to salvation. It was the same group that had been instrumental in designing and erecting the pyramids of Egypt. An integral part of that architectural spree, they claimed, was the incorporation of the "Pyramid Inch", a measure that later was permutated to reveal to an astonished world a great measure of mankind's progress: past, present and future.

Upon hearing this, Father snorted and delved into his extensive library. He emerged with the smug conclusion that the "Pyramid Inch" was a measure of expediency bearing no resemblance to *any* measure ever devised. Convinced that it was a contemporary gimmick, Father made a side trip to the liquor store, phoned George Fordyce and, in the latter's office overlooking Eighth Avenue, went to work.

After hours of mathematical planning and meticulous drafting on an enormous sheet of paper, they emerged with a scaled replica of the newly-revealed sandstone front of the Victoria Hotel.

They had worked out, in "Victoria Inches", the flood that finally beached Noah on high ground, the date and time of the final meal of the apostles and their doomed Lord, the Hundred Years War, the Industrial Revolution in England and the First World War. Everything was there prognosticated and perpetuated in the sandstone blocks from Oliver's quarry up on Seventeenth Avenue West.

Next they had to secure an audience for this revelation. They managed that too, and Father was booked to present the revelation to an audience at the next gathering of the sect.

George and Father, fortified with a modicum of scotch, unveiled the huge chart. George took his seat in the audience while, up on the stage armed with a long pointer, Father launched his talk. The "Victoria Inch", he explained, was a mystical measure capable of baring the world's history carved in Calgary sandstone. Unfortunately he was not permitted to finish his lecture due to the uproar that erupted in the ranks of the sect's faithful.

Father and George scuttled, grinning, to safety and the rest of the bottle that awaited them in a cupboard in the architect's office. The spoof had been a huge success, except for one detail: in their haste to flee the scene they had left behind the painstakingly created chart!

Reg Peach had a prankster side to his personality that delighted in outrageous schemes. Here, he and a group of soldiers, convalescing in wartime France, celebrate the New Year in high style. Peach welcomes 1918 as a sundial cautioning all sober-sides to "gather ye rosebuds whilst ye may".

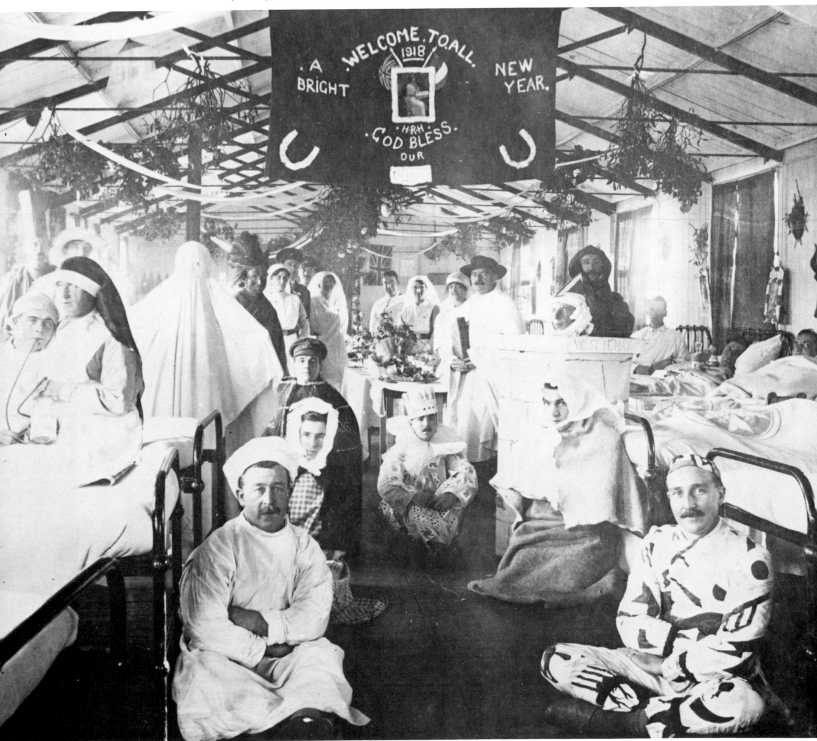

The Great 1929 Flood

by Gordon Cummings

Gordon J. Cummings was born in 1897 in Minnesota and, after immigrating to Calgary with his parents, attended Western Canada College. He received his Bachelor of Arts degree from the University of Minnesota, served briefly with the French Army during the First World War and then returned to Alberta where he eventually became President of the Western Grain Dealers' Association.

For most of his life Mr. Cummings has been actively associated with sportsmen, and in 1962 was the Alberta representative at the founding of the Canadian Wildlife Federation. He has continued that affiliation, serving as president of the federation for three years during the late 1960s, and remains actively involved to this day.

While reminiscing about Calgary in the early days, Mr. Cummings recalled the great flood of June 3, 1929 when the Elbow River rose almost eight feet in less than six hours.

My father was not a man to be taken by surprise. He had come to Calgary in 1909 deliberately seeking new markets to expand the grain merchandising business, and had spent considerable thought on prospects for our advancement. With careful planning and meticulous attention to detail he was prepared for all eventualities, so it was with much chagrin that he discovered how little he knew about the unreasonable forces of river run-off.

By 1912 Father had established himself in the Grain Exchange Building and, caught up in the real estate boom of that year, he eagerly sought out the most beautiful location in town to build a permanent home in which to settle his family. Elbow Park, with its lovely tree-shaded river and new homes, was certainly the "prestige" location, but he was somewhat suspicious of the frequent spring swells that lapped over the riverbanks. So, true to his nature, he made careful inquiries about water levels in all previous recorded years, located the Fortieth Avenue house on considerably higher ground than he felt really necessary, and, just for good measure, built an unusually high foundation.

The house was perfect; a lovely home with a large veranda and rolling lawn down to the river that was my summertime swimming hole. In those days the Elbow River wasn't dammed, so the current was fast and deep — ideal for our rafts and canoes. My mother raised a few chickens

It wasn't unusual for Fortieth Avenue to be ankle deep in springtime flood water, nor for plank sidewalks to be transformed into makeshift rafts by neighbourhood children.

in a run near the water's edge and during high water season it was my job to carry them to safety. I got pretty good at rescuing swimming chickens, and we all began to be pretty nonchalant about the annual arrival of our basement swimming pool and our floating plank sidewalks. In fact, I can remember what great fun it was to clamber to the rooftop after heavy rains or sudden thaws to watch as the river rapidly flooded its banks, but still, Father's careful calculations kept us drier than most.

It wasn't until June of 1929 that the river let him know how futile his efforts had been.

That month my parents were entertaining Mr. and Mrs. Will Spence, who had come for a visit from their home in Edmonton. Mrs. Spence was a tiny little woman who, as regent of the IODE, carried considerable stature. Her husband was as tall as my father and I'm sure equally imposing, but all dignity suffered at the whim of the elements.

The evening of their arrival was uneventful but during the night a terrific storm dumped heavy rains in the foothills, and the onrushing floods surrounded our little island of safety to the point that even my father had to admit alarm. By the time he phoned the authorities, all rescue boats had already been launched and water was lapping on to the front stairs.

A city dump cart pulled by huge horses suddenly rounded the corner, sloshed its way to the front steps and the driver gallantly offered his services. It was no time for false pride; the horses by this time were stomach-deep in the flood. Dignity suffered, but my mother and Mrs.

147

Mrs. Spence was a tiny little woman who, as regent of the IODE, carried considerable stature. Her husband was as tall as my father, and, I'm sure, equally imposing, but all dignity suffered at the whim of the elements.

Spence climbed into the huge garbage cart and peered out over the edge as the two men directed the escape in their most officious manner.

The humour of the situation may have escaped the senior Cummings, but I still laugh thinking about the naval retreat. The following year it was decided that the Glenmore Dam would be constructed to contain the spring floods. I was almost sorry to hear the news.

The Sales Pitch

by Jack Scott

In the Hungry Thirties students were doing practically anything to get money to finance their educations. Some found themselves knocking on doors trying to sell something for profit. And those who could used flattery, charm, and even cunning to make a sale.

One afternoon I heard a female voice in the outer office in debate with my secretary, trying to get in to see me without revealing the nature of her business. Presently I saw a pretty young woman in my office with her hand outstretched smiling. "Hello Mr. Scott. So you're the great rifle-shot whose picture I saw in the paper!" (I had won a competition of no great consequence.) "My father was quite a marksman. Last year he went to England on the Bisby team but I'm sure he's not in your class." (Bisby, I hasten to add, is the country's very best shooting team and certainly far above any talent of mine.)

I was not so easily flattered. "Skip the nice talk. Now what are you selling?"

"Really Mr. Scott, I'm not selling anything!" Her eyes were wide with injured innocence. "My company is bringing out a new commodity. They've chosen a few prominent businessmen to receive it for advertising purposes and you're one of those selected. I'm sure you'll be willing to pay the postage."

Aha, I thought, a pretty weak pitch after all. "No, thank you. Now please excuse me."

"Thank you for your time anyway, Mr. Scott. Perhaps next time." She turned reluctantly toward the door and, almost as an afterthought, said, "If I can tell you how many birthdays you've had, will you buy our magazine?" She was so enthusiastic I could scarcely resist her little game, so I agreed. "Fire away."

Quickly she brightened. "You, Mr. Scott, have had *one* birthday, and a *lot* of anniversaries."

I was had. With a giggle she introduced herself. "Call me Susan."

As she stepped into the outer office, I heard my secretary of many years say, "Susan, if you'll fill out the order I'll sign it for you."

The Hungry Thirties brought hard times to most of us. In this 1935 photograph, a march of United Married Men carry a placard reading, "We stand behind 12,000 on relief."

As the river lapped in over the porch and into the livingroom, the Judge sought higher ground and set up emergency rations in the second story sunroom.

Judge McCarthy

by Pat Pryde

Patricia D. Pryde is the granddaughter of Mr. Justice and Mrs. M.S. McCarthy and the daughter of Helen H. Anderson. She was raised in Vancouver and Calgary, and after attending local schools worked for Imperial Oil and Royalite Oil. Pat has generously volunteered her time and talent to the Junior Service League where her favourite placement was with the Children's Hospital. She has also served on the Vestry of Christ Church in Elbow Park, and for twelve years Pat was a governor of the board of Strathcona-Tweedsmuir School.

If ever there was a man who personified that turn of the century Calgary character, it had to be my grandfather, Maitland S. McCarthy.

Like many of the immigrant population of the new little city, "Luggy" McCarthy had been born in Ireland, and eventually made his way west after spending his youth in Ontario. Arriving in Calgary in 1902 as a young lawyer with his bride and their new baby, he quickly established himself with the political activists of the day, and within two years was elected as a Conservative Member of Parliament. His constituents were evidently pleased with his efforts because he was re-elected in 1908, and only retired from political life when he decided to accept an appointment to the Alberta Supreme Court.

The role suited him enormously. He was not only a good and fair jurist, but he had a dry wit and was popular as an after-dinner speaker. He always enjoyed a good laugh with his friend Bob Edwards of *Eye Opener* fame, so he was not without a redeeming vice or two. In fact, legend has it that during the great flood of 1929, (when my grandmother was mercifully out of town), Grandfather refused to abandon their Fortieth Avenue house. As the river lapped in over the veranda into the living room, the Judge sought higher ground and set up emergency rations in the second story sunroom where he watched the rescue manoeuvres taking place all around. Cappy Smart rowed by, directing the firemen to the cries of fleeing neighbours, but he was quickly lured away from his post to the flood party under way at the McCarthy house. There they stayed – the Judge, the Fire Chief and the Chinese help – sending only an occasional fireboat for additional supplies, until the water receded.

My grandfather was a true individualist – try as she might, my grandmother could never

152

quite civilize him. Eva McCarthy had been born "of family" back east in Ontario, and was every inch as ladylike as he was mischievous. She had worked hard to establish a neighbourhood Anglican church in Elbow Park and was delighted when at last sod was broken for its construction. Until further money could be raised for the church and chancel, the parishioners made do with the underground foundation, so the first services were held in the basement. Dignity was preserved, however, only until Grandfather, in a loud voice during his daughter's confirmation, remarked on the state of "Canon Horne's Root Cellar".

That Irish twinkle never left his eye. He left a fine family of two sons and a daughter, and happy memories to all who knew him as a friend.

Judge McCarthy — he was not only a good and fair jurist but he also had a dry wit and was popular as an after-dinner speaker.

153

Damn the Torpedoes; Full Speed Ahead!

by Donald Harvie

Donald S. Harvie was born in Calgary in 1924, the son of Eric and Dorothy (Southam) Harvie. By profession an oil company executive, Mr. Harvie also has a keen interest in Calgary's heritage. He is actively involved with The Devonian Group, the Glenbow-Alberta Institute, and Heritage Park and is a Founding Governor of Heritage Canada.

I was born on the Elbow River in 1924, grew up on its banks, and sixty years later still live on the river's cliff edge just upstream from where I first saw Calgary. It's natural then, that my memories can be closely linked to that river and that they would fall into two distinct periods: pre-dam and post-dam.

I can turn back the clock by remembering getting caught on a break-away ice flow with my chums and drifting several hundred feet in the annual spring breakup. We were terrified and probably very lucky to get ashore. I can remember watching the river rise daily during those thaws until there was no daylight under the arches of the Mission Bridge. The bridge deck itself was only held down by six large gravel-filled trucks parked on top.

I'd hurry home from Strathcona School by streetcar from Seventeenth Avenue to the turn-around at Sifton, where the water rose right to the edge of the tracks, and jump out to wait for my special fireman friend to return from a boat run.

Being small, light, agile and enthusiastic, I was his perfect mascot. Perched quietly in the boat prow, I'd hold the rope and jump out on the porch steps or veranda of a Riverdale home — tie up the boat and assist our passengers, (no more than three per load), to alight and unload groceries.

By 1931 the dam was finally built, and my father took my older sister and me on an inspection trip one afternoon into its deep, wet, dripping interior corridors and through the huge noisy turbine rooms. All the while the lake behind it flooded out Dr. McKidd's farm and changed that southwest area of our growing city. Part of the new shoreline surrounded a sixty acre point

Pre-dam perils, like riding break-away ice floes and rafting on flooded streets, ended in 1930 when construction began at the Glenmore Dam site. By 1931 the dam was finally built, and my father took my sister and me on an inspection trip one afternoon into its deep, wet, dripping interior corridors and through the huge, noisy turbine rooms.

now owned by the city. That point became Heritage Park through the efforts of my father Eric Harvie, Mayor Harry Hayes, Chief Commissioner Dudley Batchelor, and Harry Boothman, a quiet, wonderful, but effective Parks Superintendent.

Eventually I became very involved with the implementation of Heritage Park, and I well knew that an integral part of our transportation heritage was a river/lake boat. The S.S. Moyie, the ship that was chosen for reconstruction, had to satisfy our naval architects and modern safety regulations. Federal shipping approvals required three main "sea trial" tests, the final one for endurance and speed.

I remember it was the Board's monthly meeting prior to spring opening, and Bill Pratt, our no-cost-on-loan-from-Standard Gravel construction superintendent, came chuckling into the room to give us his usual optimistic progress report. "No sweat with the Moyie. All's go with the water trials." Then he added, "I had some difficulty in getting the inspector to sign off on that third endurance test. The rule book calls for a minimum three-mile straight run at full throttle, and it took some persuasion to convince him this would leave our Moyie two miles inside the Sarcee Reserve sitting alongside their school house! Since he could give me no idea about how we would ever get it back to the lake, he just signed the certificate."

An Ode to the Streetcar Era

by Ollie Kozicky

Ollie Kozicky says of her life in Calgary, "I can thank my mom and dad for being in the right place at the right time, for I was born the first daughter into a family of three sons. In 1928 I started school at St. Mary's. My first grade teacher was Miss Deborah Maloney. I clearly remember her because my dear grandfather was always threatening to 'go over and have a talk with her'. He thought she was pretty hard on me!

St. Mary's was the only Roman Catholic high school in Calgary in those days. After squeaking by there for two years and not really liking school too much, the worst possible excuse came along for me to quit. In 1939 the war broke out and I couldn't seem to concentrate on books with my brothers and childhood sweetheart going off to fight God knows where. In our wisdom my fiance and I decided to get married so we could be together until he was shipped out to parts unknown. I lived in British Columbia while my husband took his training, but that was the only time in my life I lived elsewhere than Calgary. And, all being well, I hope to end my days here."

When I was "but a slip of a girl", going for a ride on the antiquated Calgary streetcar was like buying a ticket on a midway ride. I could feel the excitement building as soon as I picked my way down to a seat while the car was in motion.

It took a well-balanced trapeze artist to keep feet on the floor. The conductor — that's what they were called then — was usually a middle-aged man that got to know his passengers through their constant use of the system. (In those days we were very lucky if there was even *one* automobile per family.) He would help older people board the trolley, and young mothers with infants and strollers in tow always got a helping hand getting on and off.

There was a big fire box right behind the conductor where a supply of coal was kept to keep the car warm during the winter. There were no shelters for patrons to huddle in from the elements to await the arrival of the friendly, hulking, weaving orange car. It was so good to hurry aboard and thaw out. But year round it was a good place to plunk down the parcels and small kids. It meant you could ride backwards and stare at all the other passengers without feeling ill mannered! There was only one large door and the step was operated by the conductor who turned a big crank of sorts; it opened the door and at the same time lowered the step. Right near this door a big box of sand was kept. If the conductor found the going tricky on some of the hills, this sand was spread on the rails to enable better traction. At that time I lived near Seventeenth Avenue and Fourteenth Street West and two very long hills merged at the bottom. If memory serves me right, more than once a run-away trolley gave the customers of Crook's Drug Store a good scare.

In the back of the car there was a neat little cubbyhole, all glassed in with a sliding door. Men (because ladies didn't in those days) could smoke in there to their hearts' content. Non-smokers wouldn't dare invade their private domain.

If you happened to board the trolley during a busy time and you were a young person or a male of any age, it was expected that you would give your seat to an older lady or gentleman. It was always a challenge to be able to stand holding on to a small handle at the top of the wicker seat, without falling headlong into the passengers' laps. A child wasn't able to hang on to one of the leather straps suspended from the top of the car. They were really dignity destroyers. You had to be prepared to call upon your sense of humour if your luck was such that you had to stand for the duration of the ride to your destination.

I'm sure the friendly conductor's patience was taxed many times on rides to and from the suburbs, when mischievous school boys would go back into the empty smoker and pull the trolley off the overhead wires. This would necessitate the conductor putting the controls into neutral, leaving his position, going outside to the back of the car and trying to place the trolley pulley back on the line — only to have the kids do it again as soon as the old car was again reaching top speed.

It now seems a miracle those old iron horses didn't jump the tracks more often. I expect that if it hadn't been for the tireless efforts of the crew of maintenance men who cared for the tracks by sweeping the switches free of gravel and debris, there would have been a lot more derailments. The cars were unique; they had three bars on the windows. I guess that was to keep the kids from falling out, or maybe to prevent the more industrious ones from boarding by a different route without paying their nickel fare. I haven't quite figured that one out, even after all these years! The floors were constructed in separate pieces with the seats positioned on a flat floor, but down the centre there were big ridges that were rather hard to navigate if you were wearing high-heeled shoes. The reasoning behind this bit of ingenuity was so that in wintertime the snow and slush brought in on passengers' boots wouldn't collect in puddles on the floor.

The system was an important link in many lives back in the good old days, and I am sure it continues to be a major part of many Calgarians' lives. I'm only sorry that technology and efficiency have replaced the romance of the streetcar era.

In the back of the car there was a neat little cubbyhole, all glassed in with a sliding door. Men (because ladies didn't in those days) could smoke in there to their hearts' content.

A trip into Calgary from the farm with the possibility of eating at a real restaurant was, in the 1930s, a thrill comparable to today's flight to London, with dinner at the Ritz. The city's eating establishments, modest by today's standards but thrilling to a small boy's palate, ranged from the Tea Kettle Inn, pictured overleaf, where ladies lunched during a busy shopping day, to the snack counter at Liggett's Drug Store shown below.

Exotic Delights

by Stan Perrott

Stanford Perrott has retired after a long career as instructor and director of the Alberta College of Art but he still keeps actively involved in Calgary's community of artists. A native Albertan, he studied at the Alberta College of Art, the Banff School of Fine Arts and in schools in Philadelphia and New York, and in 1974 he was awarded a special achievement recognition from the Alberta Government for his service in art education. Mr. Perrott has retained a child-like sensitivity to the sights and smells of exotic new surroundings, and beautifully recalls the memories of the bi-monthly treks to the big city from the family farm west of Stavely. The trip in those days took about two-and-a-half hours on dirt roads — a drive spent in delicious anticipation.

To most small boys any food tastes great, any time, anywhere. Nevertheless, a trip into Calgary from the farm with the possibility of eating at a real restaurant was, around 1930, a thrill comparable to today's flight to London with dinner at the Ritz. The air was electric with excited anticipation on those infrequent occasions when Dad packed his five children into the back seat of the 1926 McLaughlin-Buick, Mother in front, for the journey into wonderland Calgary.

Travel was slow on the difficult roads. Before long, sister Mary would lapse into dreaming of being in love with the hired man back on the farm. Brothers Wilf and John might be in a silent punching duel until little Dick began to cry from an accidental elbow-whack in the eye. But being a good lad, I, no doubt, sat quietly and mentally chose my noon menu, most often fish and chips with lots of vinegar and salt.

Somewhere in the DeWinton hills stood that piece of magic "Op-Art", the Calgary Tent and Awning billboard in the form of a tent painted so realistically that we would exclaim, "Look John, some crazy man has pitched his tent away out here in the wild hills!" When John realized the illusion had fooled him, another punching match would follow, with Dad threatening to "turn right round and go home!"

The sight of the Big Horn Brewery in Manchester, southern outpost of the city, brought us all to order; hair was smoothed, clothes straightened and cookie crumbs brushed onto the floor. We were all ready for lunch at Bartlett's.

It was a fine restaurant. Frank Bartlett's Old English Fish and Chips was located on the

west side of Centre Street between Seventh and Eighth Avenues. We were oblivious to decor. Fine meant good taste and strange new odors. Service was cordial; well adapted to country folk. High-backed wooden booths lined the walls back from the cashier's pulpit. Surely this was Calgary's first "take-out" restaurant. It was ingeniously equipped. We children were intrigued by what resembled a pulley clothes line stretching above our heads from the front counter to the kitchen in the rear. A metal basket suspended from pulleys mounted above and below the two wires was put into motion when the front waitress pulled the wires apart by drawing on an arm-length lever. To the back of the restaurant travelled the basket when the customer gave his order. The waitress would then "get on the blower", indeed blowing into a tube which, like the clothes line, reached to the kitchen but by a route along the walls. Orders spoken into the tube were miraculously heard in the kitchen and shortly thereafter the basket bearing fish and chips wrapped in newspaper ran along the wires to the cashier's area for delivery to the waiting customers.

Bartlett's is now but a memory. You can't find fish and chips made like Bartlett's used to, and even the vinegar seems to have changed. Did we have dessert? I can't recall but it doesn't matter. It was the fish and chips that were the grand thrill.

The twilight ride back to the farm was cosy, providing rain hadn't turned the road north of High River into a bog. The smallest boys slept while the rest of us played "I Spy."

Isn't it strange that the game we adults now play is "I remember"? Those childhood adventures must have been the best times.

M.M. Porter Aids and Abets Social Credit

by M.M. Porter

The Honourable M.M. Porter, who served as a judge of the Appellate Division of the Supreme Court of Alberta from 1954 to 1969, was born in 1894 and was called to the Alberta Bar in 1919. He practised law in the early years with J.E. Brownlee, who became UFA Premier of Alberta in 1925, and later with The Honourable Gordon H. Allen and Ross MacKimmie, who now heads the law firm.

Guillespie Hanna, who farmed near Carstairs, Alberta, had been a longtime friend and client of mine when he retired to live in Calgary. He became a member of a local Baptist church and one day came to consult me about a church problem. He said that a lay preacher, by the name of William Aberhart, a blustery gentleman who taught high school for a living, was serving in the pulpit of the church. He alleged that Aberhart was departing from the creed of the church and was appealing to a substantial number of its members. Hanna wanted the services in that church to follow the creed of the Baptist Church and wished to know if the orthodox members – those that adhered to the creed – could do anything to put a stop to Aberhart's activities.

I was unable to tell him without having a look at the law. I did some research, though, and found a duplicate of the experience in the case of the Presbyterian Church in Scotland. In the old Scottish case the members who adhered to the creed brought an action in court to determine whether they could expel those who did not adhere to the creed. The case went all the way to The House of Lords which decided that, when there is a division among the adherents of a church, those who follow the creed succeed to the church and all its properties, and those who refuse to follow the creed are in the church on sufferance.

I was able, therefore, to tell Mr. Hanna that Mr. Aberhart could not continue if the adherents of the creed objected to his presence. I wrote Mr. Hanna a letter setting out this opinion which he in due course delivered to Mr. Aberhart, who left the church.

Aberhart later formed the Prophetic Bible Institute. His congregation grew to great numbers and ultimately he built a church on Eighth Avenue. His adherents filled the new Institute, and public demand instigated the radio sermons that were heard by the whole of the population covered by CFCN's broadcast area. It was a phenomenal station which then broadcast on a wave length of 1010. This gave almost complete coverage to the whole of Alberta, south of Peace River. His listening congregation grew to such numbers that he was known to nearly everyone in the province.

Times were tough. Everyone was in trouble and could see no way out. Low prices, drought, high interest rates, all of the faults of the Depression were pressing in on the people. Many of them found hope in Aberhart's sermons because he defined for them the cause of their troubles, naming the big shots, the banks, the railroads and the money system. The fact that he gave simplistic answers to complex issues only made him more popular, and, as so often happens, when one pretends to diagnose the disease he becomes the person who seems capable of curing it.

Unfortunately Mr. Aberhart heard of Social Credit, a monetary theory evolved by an Englishman named Douglas. To the economically naive, Social Credit seemed like a timely prescription to cure the ills of Alberta. Aberhart, embracing the philosophy as the elixir for our problems, promised each Alberta resident a monthly dividend of twenty-five dollars, and his audience became almost universal throughout the province.

He did his best to persuade the UFA Government then in power to adopt Social Credit, but by then Albertans were anxious for a new slate. So Aberhart's movement became a political party and won the 1935 election, even though Aberhart did not run for a seat. He took the leadership after the party's victory and became Premier.

Aberhart passed all sorts of curious legislation. He repudiated the provincial debt. He cut the interest on the savings deposits of the people who banked with the old Alberta Government Savings Branch. He passed a statute headed the Horizontal Debt Cut Act. All of Canada became frightened by the seeming irresponsibility and futility of Aberhart's government.

In this state of affairs I was asked by a client to go to Edmonton to meet the Cabinet to deal with some matter then pending between my client and the government. I had not, until then, met Mr. Aberhart, although I certainly knew him by reputation.

The Cabinet met in the council chamber and I was asked to join them. Mr. Aberhart rose in his place to introduce me, and he did this by saying, "But for this young man I would not be here." He explained that his experience in the Baptist Church had given him the evangelical impetus to go on a path which culminated in his revelations about Social Credit. I, of course, had hurried his pilgrimage along!

Premier Aberhart and the members of his Cabinet, and I myself, enjoyed the incident and he often laughed with me about it later on. But I must add that his famous "hit list" of big shots and bankers often included people who were my clients, and, even though I was guilty only by association, my involvement in Social Credit's temporary success often weighed heavily on my conscience.

William Aberhart broadcasting one of his famous radio sermons. CFCN's broadcast area covered almost the whole province south of the Peace River and his listening congregation virtually included the entire population of Alberta.

Once Upon a Saturday Afternoon

by Ollie Kozicky

When we were little girls during the early 1930s, it was a marvelous treat for me and my younger sister to go downtown on the rickety old streetcar. We loved it, especially in the winter when we could stand close to the coal bin and feel the warmth of the old stove that the conductor stoked up every two or three blocks. The ride was a wonderful beginning to an exciting adventure, and it always started with a visit to the most glamorous place in the world.

Woolworth's sat in splendour on Eighth Avenue between the Bay and Eaton's, but to get there from the corner where our Number Seven streetcar stopped, we had to pass the guys hanging out by Helmer's Poolhall, and the brush with danger always made us squirm. Once inside, however, the magic of the glittering "gems" transported us to sheer ecstacy. The smells of freshly made popcorn and squeaky oiled floors wafted by us as we wished over each treasure, trying to stretch our tiny nickels just a little farther. Those coins were pinched many times before we finally handed them to the saleslady, but I don't ever remember being in the least disappointed by our choices.

Then, fairly dancing with the excitement of the day's transactions, we tumbled over one another in our race down to the new post office on Eighth Avenue East, always approaching with apprehension, hoping that the lady who sold stamps would be wearing her long dangling earrings that flip-flopped everytime she moved her head. And then, errands finished, we hurried along, because if we had time we could stop in at Jimmie's for an ice cream soda.

Of course everyone knew it was really called The Palace of Eats, but to us children, who had to push through the adults waiting there out of the cold for their transit connections, it was just Jimmie's. No one was ever hurried along to make way for paying customers; we drank our sodas alongside the dozens of people who were there just for the visit.

Regretfully the afternoon grew short and it was time to find our little yellow streetcar tickets for the ride home. We tucked them in our mitts for safekeeping, adjusted our bundles and scarves, and headed outside for one last look at the Saturday afternoon bustle of the big city. The policeman in his high hat whistled to signal that we could cross the street, and we were off at a run for a quick visit with the man who ran the elevator in the Herald Building. He always had a joke for us, and, even though he knew we had no business in the building, he gave us a ride to the top floor. Then, giggling all the way, we jumped the steps two and three at a time on our way down, joyfully aware that no teacher was there to remind us to walk properly.

Too soon we could see the Number Seven approaching to pick us up for the trip back up Fourteenth Street. We settled in our seats though, scratching a window through the frost on the glass to see if the old bucket of bolts would make it up the icy rails. Holding our breath to urge it along, I suspect we thought if we dared move the climb would fail, and we would have to retreat all the way to the corner again for another attempt. That never happened — sheer good luck, I guess.

The Palace of Eats across from the Bay.

Governor Sale: Prophet of The H.B.C.

by M.M. Porter

The Hudson's Bay Company owes its success in large measure to Charles Sale. He was a man of vision who recognized that a seemingly insignificant trend must necessarily alter the merchandising philosophy of the Company in western Canada, but his observations were hooted down by the English Board of Directors and he was discharged for his troubles.

The Hudson's Bay Company was operated by a board of directors, almost all of whom lived in England. Policy was determined by this board as it had been since 1670, and no one seemed of a mind to change with the times until the cataclysm of the Depression when Charles Sale became Governor of the Company. Sale, a world trader in his own right, recognized that the upheaval of 1929 had made the old rules of economic order anachronistic. No longer could the Bay depend largely on the fur trade. If it was to survive the new order, it must adjust to change.

Shown here just prior to the stock market crash of 1929, the Hudson's Bay store in Calgary had begun construction on a large addition to the south side of the building, but it was not until 1955 that further expansion took place along the west side.

After reviewing the Company's operations in Canada, Sale called a meeting of the Canadian Committee in Winnipeg to discuss his observations and to announce what his recommendations would be to the English Board. And, because I was the Company's solicitor in Calgary at that time, I was invited to attend, along with other solicitors and various store managers.

His proposal was shocking. With little ado he outlined his plan for a major expansion of the retail operation in western Canada. He wanted to build new stores in Winnipeg, Edmonton and Vancouver and to continue construction on a large addition to the store in Calgary that had begun prior to the '29 crash. However, to this committee of responsible, upstanding Canadian businessmen who were only too aware of the economic conditions in western Canada, the idea was appalling. Business was suffering terribly; it was no time to even consider expansion; their opposition was unanimous. Sale persisted and said that he intended to take his proposal to the Board in England regardless of the Canadian decision, but minds were closed and the meeting ended.

I was intrigued by the man; I knew him to be an intelligent, thoughtful person with a great fund of experience world wide, and I was anxious to know what had brought him to such a proposal. So, following dinner that evening, I asked to meet with him for a chat about the day's activities, and he agreed.

The Governor was cordial and encouraged me to speak out even though I had no real footing to discuss the programme. In response to my obvious question, he explained that his job as head of the Hudson's Bay Company was to ensure that the Company made money fifty years hence. And, therefore, the responsibility for the present earnings, in the interim, lay with his predecessors who had not done a job that resulted in the success the Company should be enjoying. "Their mistake," he said, "was in not realizing that the advent of the closed, heated car meant the end of the fur business." Eatons, on the other hand, had capitalized on western Canadian markets by supplying rural customers' needs through catalogue sales which guaranteed the business

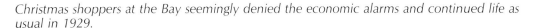

Christmas shoppers at the Bay seemingly denied the economic alarms and continued life as usual in 1929.

of the now-expanding urban population. The Bay should have recognized those trends and been ready to profit by them. "Instead," he went on, "the great American trading companies will no doubt soon invade our territory in western Canada. My plan is to *over*build to the point where any potential invader will be shut out, at least until the Company has modernized and improved its merchandising methods."

Of course he knew that he would be criticized, at home and in Canada both, for expending sums in excess of what were needed to take care of the current trade potential, but again he emphasized that his job was to build for a sound position fifty years down the road. He said, "You will live to see the Hudson's Bay Company prospering beyond our dreams with the future of this country because my programme will preserve the territory."

He was right on both counts. He was not only criticized, he was removed from office. But now that those fifty years have proved him right, one hopes that he lived long enough to have seen with some satisfaction those trends progress toward his prophecy.

Georgina Thomson

by Frances Coulson

During the three year period from 1930 to 1933 in Depression-ridden Calgary, the Calgary Public Library did a roaring business. The Main Library (it had only one branch then) was that fine sandstone building at Third Street and Twelfth Avenue Southwest, now renamed Memorial Park Library. From nine a.m. until nine-thirty p.m., an unending procession of men, women and children filed through the library's main entrance for the best and least expensive recreation in town.

Times were hard. Many Calgarians were unemployed; others were suffering salary cutbacks. Small businesses were struggling to keep afloat. With little money to spend, people were looking for inexpensive ways to fill their leisure time. The library provided the ideal solution. People read avidly, some for recreation, many for information and education. This was the heyday of the debating club, the literary club and current events group. Readers were searching for the answers to economic and political problems. Books on Communism, Fascism, Naziism and the political philosophy of Major Douglas' Social Credit were in great demand, and, either because of economic necessity or a desire to fill leisure time with useful arts and crafts, the do-it-yourself manual became immensely popular.

The heart of the library was a small north room with an even smaller room attached to it. This was the Reference Department, and its presiding genius was a short, red-haired Scottish-Canadian girl with bright blue eyes and a pawky wit. Georgina Thomson ("Georgie" to her many friends) possessed a formidable intelligence, infinite resourcefulness, sensitivity and empathy for all humanity — especially the underdog. Georgie Thomson provided answers to an incredible number of questions. Debaters depended on her, women's and men's clubs deferred to her, and clerics besieged her for inspiration for sermons. Business and professional people asked for and received help; nothing was too much trouble for her and everyone from the most influential citizen to the least significant of the have-nots got the same service.

One particular day an urgent phone call came from the offices of the legal firm of Bennett, Hannah and Sanford. Would the librarian look up an item in Hansard, the House of Commons record, for The Honourable R.B. Bennett? ("R.B.", as he was popularly known in Calgary, his political bailiwick, was at that time Prime Minister of Canada.) Miss Thomson quickly located the passage and typed it out. A little later the great man himself arrived to pick up the information. He read and approved the item, and, reaching into his pocket, he pulled out a dollar and proffered it to Miss Thomson, "for your trouble". Miss Thomson blushed to the roots of her hair and put her hands behind her back. "I don't take money from patrons for helping them." R.B., completely taken aback, pocketed the money, thanked her and left. It was the first time Georgie had been offered payment for services rendered, and undoubtedly it was one of the few times that R.B. had had such an offer rejected!

Georgina Thomson's name is familiar to many Calgarians who never knew her. The branch library that carries her name perpetuates her tradition of generosity and love of learning, and the book she wrote about her family's homesteading days in southern Alberta, *Crocus and Meadowlark Country*, makes vivid the history of the pioneers.

Bishop L. Ralph Sherman

by Joan Weir

Joan Weir, a Canadian author and historian, was born and brought up in Calgary. Educated at Elbow Park School and St. Hilda's School for Girls, she moved to Winnipeg with her family in 1943. She graduated from the University of Manitoba with a Bachelor of Arts degree in English and subsequently took creative writing at the University of Indiana.

She is the author of five juvenile novels, including So I'm Different, Career Girl, and The Secret At Westwind. She has written two adult histories: The History Of Walhachin, and The Caledonians. A biography of her father and a selection of his sermons has been published by the Anglican Book Centre entitled Sherman. In addition she has written three plays for children's theatre and a number of short stories.

Ralph Sherman came to Calgary during the late 1920s as the new Anglican bishop. He was just forty years old, the youngest man ever to have been elected to the Canadian House of Bishops. He believed that religion was bigger than rules, or denominations, or ritual. He brought with him a new image of what a religious leader should be. "You'll never see another tree!" they warned him in eastern Canada as he set out for the diocese of Calgary, but he didn't believe them. Nor would he have worried if it had been true. He would have imported some seedlings and started his own forest.

One day in 1933, a burial service was held in St. Mary's Roman Catholic Cathedral for Father William Edwin Cameron, first principal of St. Mary's High School. In those days ecumenism was unknown; each religious denomination fought to maintain its own absolute identity, and it was a rare thing for anyone to attend the service of another congregation. But Sherman merely pulled his scarf up to hide his clerical collar and purple stock, and sat in the pews with the rest of the mourners.

Several weeks later the following item appeared in *The Western Catholic Reporter*: ". . . No prie-dieu was set out for Bishop Sherman, and no acknowledgement was made of his presence. Not many were even aware that an Anglican Bishop was present, much less why he was there. But Bishop Sherman had come to remember, before God, a man who had been his friend and fellow Rhodes' Scholar at Oxford, twenty-odd years before."

It was Bishop Ralph Sherman who planned, organized and preached Calgary's first church

Ralph Sherman, second from left, at his installation as Anglican Bishop of Calgary in 1928. At forty he was the youngest man ever elected to the Canadian House of Bishops.

radio broadcast. Radios were placed in every Anglican church throughout the city so the entire congregation could hear the Bishop's message from the Pro-Cathedral.

It was the custom at the Cathedral for one of the young servers to turn off the lights in the chancel as soon as the sermon began, and then on again when it was over. Unfortunately no one had warned the server on that particular day that the radio hook-up was on the same switch as the lights.

It came time for the sermon; the lights dimmed and then shut off, and the Bishop began his address. First he greeted every rector and parish by name, then he gave a stirring twenty minute talk. When the sermon was finished, there was a hymn, and the usual closing prayer.

But, just as the service was ending, a note was delivered to John Blewett, then curate at the Cathedral. With some misgivings Blewett passed it on to the Bishop.

The Bishop was furious. Surely, he insisted, someone from the radio station must have realized what had happened. Surely *someone* could have telephoned, or driven round before the entire service was over! And, without even pausing to shake hands at the church door, he stormed the few blocks to the radio station.

The radio operators, whose job it was to monitor the broadcast, were there all right, but they weren't monitoring anything. They weren't even aware that anything had gone wrong because they were all seated around a table playing poker. "The wrath of God" undoubtedly had new meaning that Sunday afternoon because subsequent broadcasts were conducted without a hitch.

A Child's Garden of Memories

by Joan Weir

When I was little, in the 1930s and '40s, we lived down by the Elbow River in a huge stone house that was owned by the Anglican Church, and among my favourite memories are the long skates we used to take up that river in the winter.

What sticks most in my mind is not so much the skating, or the crisp cold Alberta days, or the Christmas-card scenery with hoar frost coating the trees edging the river, but rather that delicious "tempting-fate" sensation that invariably swept over me as suddenly, in the distance, I would see a line of water flowing toward us over top of the ice. It would be a signal for my father to tell us to turn around and head back, and I for one would turn in panic. I knew that the depth of water would be scarcely more than an inch — that it was just a controlled overflow being allowed to escape through the dam to equalize the pressure — but for a small unsteady skater, the necessity for staying ahead of that relentlessly advancing wall of water provided a challenge as great as that faced by any explorer who had ventured into the Canadian wilderness.

Of course to a child each season has its highlights and, in Calgary, summer means Stampede. In those days the Stampede ran for just a week. It started on a Monday, the second Monday in July, and on the preceding day the brightly coloured coaches bearing the equipment for the midway shows would arrive in town. Shortly after noon the first of them could be spotted coming down Seventeenth Avenue and turning into the Stampede Grounds.

Our stone house by the river, just a block and a half away, was the perfect vantage point. Right after church my brother and I would take up our positions on the lawn, for it was our self-appointed task to count the vehicles. Each year we kept track. The record — I can't remember now which year it occurred — was two hundred and twelve. We refused to be lured into abandoning our vantage point for any reason, because we knew the count had to be exact, for that was the criterion by which the true success or failure of the Stampede was reckoned. It didn't matter how large the total attendance might be during the six days that followed, or how loud the applause at the evening performances. It didn't matter even if a new time record was set in the famous chuckwagon races. The true success or failure of each Stampede was determined by the total number of brightly decorated coaches that drove into town that Sunday afternoon, bearing the equipment and trappings to bring the week-long event to life. However, I suspect now that maybe my brother and I were the only people in all of Calgary who realized that.

Those childhood summers in Calgary are long past now, but there is a special memory that is undoubtedly shared by many of my generation who will smile in recalling their picnics at St. George's Island. In those days there were no protective fences around the huge concrete prehistoric animals at the park, and we delighted in climbing about their enormous legs and scampering up the long tails. But the best picnic of all was the one interrupted by a sudden summer squall. That meant we could all dash for cover under the enormous dinosaur and watch the rain torrent around us. And somehow, to me at least, standing safe and dry under the huge body brought home more vividly than any history book the sense of what it must have been like to have lived in an age when such creatures roamed the earth.

When I was little we used to go for long skates up the Elbow River and pass by hoar-frosted trees that made our neighbourhood look like a winter scene from a Christmas card.

Dr. R.B. Deane

by Gordon Townsend

Dr. Gordon Townsend describes himself as a hybrid Canadian. He was born in New Brunswick, grew up in Saskatchewan, graduated in Medicine from McGill in Montreal, and now makes his home in Alberta. Specializing in orthopaedic surgery, he is a Fellow of The Royal College of Surgeons of Canada and of The International College of Surgeons.

My predecessor, Dr. Reginald Burton Deane, was not only the first orthopaedic surgeon in Calgary, but also the first in the province of Alberta. His family had played a founding role in the political history of the province; his father had been an inspector serving with Colonel Macleod and his sister was the wife of Inspector Alexander Primrose, who for a brief period had been Lieutenant-Governor of Alberta. It was therefore only natural that his interest in provincial politics would be acute.

Dr. Deane was in every respect a gentleman of the old school, with a wide ranging intelligence. Since he had a profound knowledge of the English language (and most of its allied profanities) and being a man of strong opinion and vigorous assertion, he was known to enjoy a lively debate at considerable volume. His colleagues became accustomed to instrument-rattling discussions and regarded him with amused tolerance. Even his nurse, a gentle motherly soul, evidently suffered the debates with good humour because she worked at his side for forty years or more.

Not long before Dr. Deane died in the late 1930s, during one of the better intervals in his long struggle to survive his last illness, he was being visited by his friend, Dr. John McEachern. Dr. Deane was propped up in bed, half dozing; his long-time nurse sat quietly knitting in a chair at the end of his bed, and the discussion came around to the subject of Alberta's new political party. Social Credit had been in power only a few years, but already the radical new economic theories had created serious problems and Dr. Deane had lost a great deal of money.

Not meaning to create undue excitement, Dr. McEachern only mentioned the name of the new premier in passing on the way to less emotional topics. But the flag had been dropped. Dr. Deane raised himself from his pillow, eyes blazing! "That God-Damned-Son-of-a-Bitch!" Whereupon his nurse dropped her knitting, jumped up from her chair and exclaimed, "Oh Dr. Deane! You're feeling *better!*"

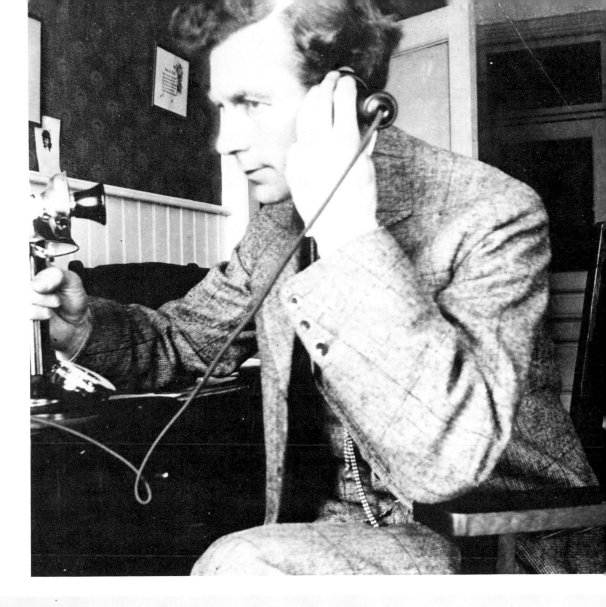

Dr. R.B. Deane, Calgary's first orthopaedic surgeon came from a family that had played a founding role in the political history of the province. Here he is pictured in his office using the telephone and on his rounds in his horse drawn buggy.

In 1926 the Colonel Belcher Hospital moved to a warehouse called the Blow Building. Located on Eighth Avenue West, it was an inadequate set-up with pretty rustic facilities.

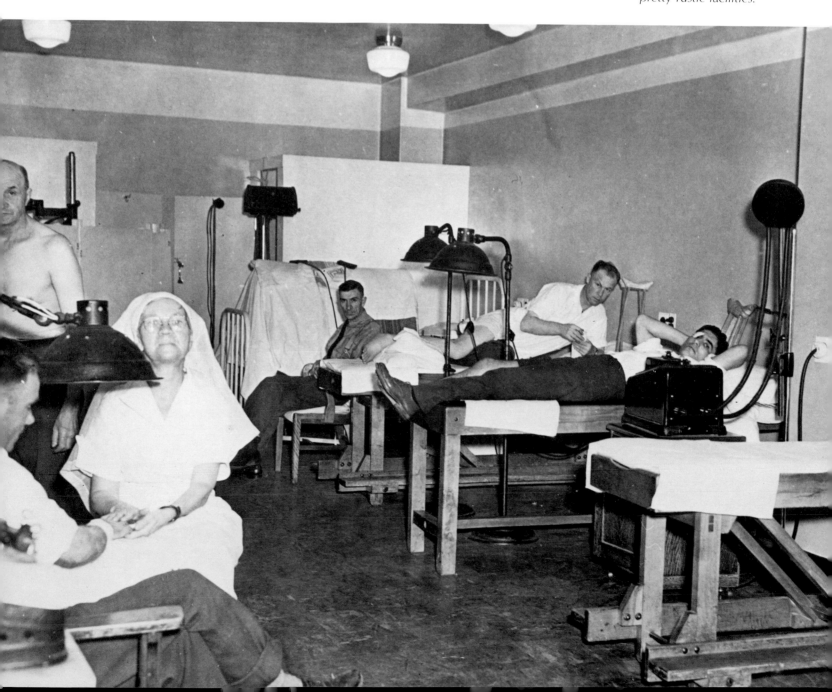

Nursing Student Days in Pre-war Calgary

by Ruth Rothel

Ruth (Grainge) Rothel was born in Calgary of parents who had homesteaded in the Hand Hills area. She graduated from the General Hospital School of Nursing and, after nursing assignments in Ponoka and other small Alberta communities, returned to Calgary where she worked with the staff of the

Colonel Belcher Hospital from 1940 to 1959.

Mrs. Rothel passed away in April, 1984. This excerpt from her memoirs, however, can be shared by many from the medical community who had similar experiences to her's during wartime in Calgary.

I can't say that I grew up wanting to be a nurse, but in 1936 it seemed like a smart move, considering the hard times. Just before I went into training, in fact, I was a very faint-hearted witness to a wood splitting accident that severed a young boy scout's finger. I was long gone by the time anyone else reacted to the emergency and I didn't re-appear until the all clear sounded. But I swallowed my fear and entered nursing school where, very quickly, I was too busy to think about being queasy at the sight of blood.

We were captive students — in order to take advantage of free room and board, plus the salary of eleven dollars a month, we faced a six-and-a-half day week of hard work with extra lectures that were invariably scheduled on that free half day. The work was back-breaking, and we were lucky if *all* we laboured were the prescribed hours. Very often overtime added additional hours to that schedule. Worse still was the night duty tour that lasted for four to six weeks at a stretch: seven p.m. to seven a.m. seven nights a week — eighty-four hours a week — provided, of course, we got off duty on time! Naturally, we were all exhausted by this routine, but no one dared take a sick day, because every missed day of training had to be accounted for, and was added on to the term at the end of the year.

Finally, in the third year, our salaries went up to sixteen dollars a month. With free room and board, that seemed like a lot of money and we looked forward with great anticipation to graduation and a real job.

179

It was 1940 when I was taken on as the thirteenth nurse on the staff of the Colonel Belcher Hospital. At that time the army was making do with temporary facilities in a warehouse called the Blow Building, so we had to get by with pretty rustic facilities. The convalescing soldiers made their own beds and some would help the orderlies sweep floors, carry trays, change the drinking water and generally help the staff cope with the inadequate set-up.

Two years later the Federal Government finally purchased Senator Patrick Burns' home. A temporary isolation hospital was immediately opened in the house and I was assigned to be night nurse. The job, I thought, was easy though pretty futile. There were only two patients: one upstairs with the measles, the other downstairs with chicken pox. I'm afraid that before they left each had both!

Decorating the ward for Christmas at the old Colonel Belcher Hospital in the Blow Building, late 1920s.

We got busier though, and more rooms filled until one patient even had to be housed in the dining room. As we were examining him after his admittance, he appeared to be quite nervous. Alarmed, he questioned us about the seriousness of his illness. We assured him that his was a minor problem, but he was not to be fooled. "What then," he quavered, "am I doing in the dying room?"

180

During the Second World War, the Federal Government purchased Senator Patrick Burns' home and a temporary isolation hospital was immediately opened in the house.

The Samaritan Club

by Joyce Williams

Joyce (Yorath) Williams has been a home-maker and active volunteer all of her adult life. She has donated her time to the Calgary Red Cross, the United Fund and to the Samaritan Club. She recalls her early family life with fondness.

"My father (C.J. Yorath), mother and two brothers came to Canada from London, England in 1913. As City Manager of both Saskatoon and Edmonton, Dad became well known and highly respected as an able administrator and, in 1925, became President of North West Utilities in Edmonton and Canadian Western Natural Gas Company in Calgary. In November of that year we moved to Calgary, and lived on Prospect Avenue where I can remember my parents entertaining at large lavish parties. I wasn't allowed to be downstairs with the adults of course, but I do recall peering over the bannister at the top of the stairs, raining ping pong balls down onto the guests below."

In 1935 the Junior Samaritan Club was formed. We were twelve in all, daughters of the senior Samaritans who had organized during the First World War in Calgary, as a charitable society helping individuals and organizations in need. We assisted our mothers in their money-raising projects and in their activities. Within two years though, the seniors decided they were ready to retire, and felt they could hand over the reins to the juniors. They stayed on as associate members however, always ready with helpful advice and assistance.

Our primary fund raisers were the two annual rummage sales in the spring and fall, and the legendary Terrill's Chrysanthemum Tea held during the Christmas season.

The tea was the major event of the social season, and Terrill's Green Houses on Ninth Avenue East were our hosts. Women came from all corners of the city and all walks of life — all dressed to the nines in hats, veils and gloves — ready to support a worthy cause and bolster their own sagging holiday larders with our home baked products.

The logistics of staging such an event were tremendous, and the staff of Terrill's was more than helpful. An enormous area adjacent to the office was cleared so that tables and chairs could be set up, and along the north wall we stationed long tables of baked goods and handicraft items. Unfortunately our only source of water came from cold water taps in two large laundry sinks,

182

so employees were kept busy transferring kettles of water from sinks to hot plates to tea tables. The china was rented, but we girls ransacked our homes for tea services, trays, cake and sandwich plates and tablecloths.

A long line awaited when the doors opened each year. Most quickly bought their home baking and handicrafts and then toured the greenhouses full of chrysanthemums and poinsettias. After having a cup of tea they would leave, making room for the others waiting their turn.

We did have one notable exception however. Every year the same four elderly ladies were first in line — always arrayed in the hats they had bought at the fall rummage sale. They would rush to their favourite table with the best viewing point and there they stayed until closing time. Never did they refuse a re-fill of their tea cups or another sweet, but they were a cheerful lot and we would have missed them terribly if they'd failed to show up at the annual event.

Mrs. William Arden, Mrs. J.H. Woods and Mrs. Eddie Taylor, members of the original Samaritan Club, collect bottles and cans for the First World War POW Fund.

The Royal Visit of 1939

by Marguerite Langille

On May 26, 1939, King George VI and Queen Elizabeth paid a brief visit to Calgary. It was the first time that a reigning monarch had come to Canada, and people all across the land greeted them with a hearty, enthusiastic welcome.

The school children were given a holiday in order to see the parade, and I was with a group of teachers from Langevin Junior High School who met on Crescent Road Northwest, and stood with some of our pupils to watch the proceedings.

It was a beautiful, sunny day, and there was an atmosphere of great excitement as onlookers gathered along the sidewalk to wait for the procession. Flags were flying, and many residences on the parade route were decorated for the occasion. One of these, the home of Mr. and Mrs. Norman Kennedy, on Tenth Avenue and First Street Northwest, was gaily trimmed with hand-sewn, red, white, and blue pennants festooning the eaves.

Cheers in the distance alerted the spectators that the parade was really coming. Soon the limousines reached us, and, for a brief ecstatic moment, we caught a glimpse of Their Majesties waving to the crowd.

However, they were driven by so quickly that we felt slightly disappointed and wondered how we could get another view. Mr. John Bryne, one of the Langevin teachers who had his car nearby, had a sudden brillant idea. Since the royal party was to take the train west for Banff directly after the parade, three of us could go in the car with Mr. and Mrs. Bryne and their two little girls, and drive quickly to the Bowness siding near the Baker Sanitarium. The train was to slow down there for a brief pause and, hopefully, there would be an unscheduled appearance of the royal couple.

We raced west to Bowness and were well rewarded for the effort. The King and Queen stepped out on the platform at the back of the train and we were standing beside the tracks just a few feet away. The two little Bryne girls were waving their flags vigorously, Mr. Verge, our school principal, was bowing most respectfully, King George waved, and Queen Elizabeth looked directly at our party with a most dazzling, radiant smile.

Now, forty-five years later as I write about this episode, Dorothy Hawley, the other teacher present in 1939, thinks Queen Elizabeth was smiling toward Mr. Verge's unusually low respectful bows but I have always thought Her Majesty smiled at the two little girls waving their flags. At any rate, we all went home with happy memories, and, even after all these years, none of us will ever forget that very gracious smile.

Facing Page: *We knew the train was to slow for a brief pause, and we hoped we might catch a glimpse of the royal couple. We raced west to catch the train, and were rewarded for our efforts when Queen Elizabeth smiled at us.*

In 1939 King George and Queen Elizabeth visited Calgary on a cross-country tour and were honoured at a reception at the Stampede grounds where fur rugs carpeted the procession.

186

The Mounted Constabulary

by Jack Farish

Jack Farish came to Calgary in 1927 from his native England after hearing about the fabled Stampede. As a twenty-one year old farmer's son, he entered the farm machinery business until the Depression brought an end to that kind of venture. He then began working in the general insurance field and settled into Canadian life.

It was his life long love for winter sports that introduced him to river skating the year he arrived in Calgary. Mr. Farish tells of skating up the Elbow River as far as the Weaselhead that winter. "A party of us young fellows decided to have a day's outing so we arranged a rendezvous with the girls. If they would supply the picnic, we would pack the luncheon sandwiches and cakes in our ruck sacks for the five-mile journey. One young lady, however, decided to treat us and she arrived with a freshly-baked, juicy apple pie! None of us minded the fact that it couldn't be backpacked — we took turns carrying it flat in our hands, enjoying the delicious warm smell that hurried us along to our winter picnic spot."

Those young friends were mature adults by September of 1939 however, when Calgary mobilized for war. Most were ineligible for active duty because of age, although eager to participate, so, when the call came for volunteers to offer their time and talents to the cause, they enthusiastically responded, and Mr. Farish became a member of the Mounted Constabulary.

At the outbreak of the Second World War Calgary had quickly become a training centre with army barracks at Mewata and Sarcee, and a navy depot at HMCS Tecumseh, but it was the mounted militia that needed the volunteers to patrol the home front each night. There was a real feeling of ominous, ever-present threat during those years in Calgary; we were only a short fifty miles away from the POW camp at Kananaskis and many Calgarians thought it entirely possible that a prisoner might escape and sabotage the city's water supply. But for most of us in the Mounted Constabulary, the home front was a place of high adventure and good fellowship.

Unique to Calgary was the Mounted Constabulary. These middle-aged men patrolled the hills from dusk till

dawn, and the citizens of Calgary slept more soundly knowing the Constabulary was keeping watch.

Led by Troop Commander Eric Harvie, the Mounted Constabulary rides out.

We even paid for the privilege! We supplied our own horses, though the military did provide tack, and we willingly volunteered our time two nights a week to drill our horses to load by truck, eight at a time. If ever an escape did occur, it was reasoned that men on horseback would be needed to bushwhack into the rough back country of the Kananaskis. We trained just east of Cochrane and down around the Red Deer Lake area, and on a rotating schedule two of us patrolled the shores of the Glenmore Reservoir each night — on the lookout for that hypothetical German chemist armed with his vial of deadly poison.

As an adjunct to the local police, we in the militia were led by Chief Dave Ritchie. There were fifty of us mounted on horseback, in addition to the hundred or so on foot — all of us fit for service but just beyond the age where we could enlist for active duty. Some of us on horseback got a little soft though, because I remember that when Chief Ritchie died and all of us formed an honour guard to march the several miles from the church to the cemetery, those riding boots proved unworthy of *any* kind of infantry duty.

When the war ended we of course thankfully disbanded, but I think all of us miss the camaraderie of those years. It was exhilarating knowing that we could serve in a time of need and our morale stayed high throughout.

190

The Calgary Sketch Club

by Janet Mitchell

The best thing about the Calgary Sketch Club in the early 1940s was its location. From a bird's eye view overlooking Eighth Avenue between First and Second Streets West, we young artists were witness to the bustle of the city about its business. We watched the constant parade of servicemen, the ordinary citizens on rounds of errands, and the flow of street car traffic all pulsing with the heart beat of wartime.

All of us were caught up with the tension and excitement of the era, and, for those of us who were young and intensely aware of the drama, it was a time of soul searching over endless

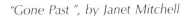

"Gone Past", by Janet Mitchell

cups of coffee. We could quit our easels and sketch pads to adjourn downstairs to Picardy's or over to the White Lunch, and sit all night around the big round table where, for the price of a ten cent coffee, we could argue endlessly, bubbling over with creative enthusiasm. It was the exchange of ideas that nurtured us.

Although all of us in those days thought we had the potential for greatness and were ambitious in our pursuit of fame, some of us were actually paid for our talents. Jimmy Bird had his advertising display workshop in our building and kept busy churning out the billboards that advertised the twice weekly change of movies at the Capital Theatre across the street. And Ernie King, across the hall, ran his tailoring establishment. The minute Ernie appeared in his cream flannel suit and straw bowler we knew that spring had arrived once more.

Most of us, though, were visual artists and we clung together for mutual support and inspiration. We did what we could to furnish the sketch club to make it as comfortable as possible, but finally it was decided that what we all needed was a bit of humour to lighten the atmosphere. A party was planned. The ticket for admission would be one personalized cartoon to decorate the studio wall.

Now we were a mixed bag of personalities, but Matt Lindstrom stood out as one of the more humourless of the lot. He was a dour Finn who had emigrated during the Depression and probably saw little that he considered laughable, but he had considerable talent. So, when he appeared at the party with the funniest cartoons of all, he was the hands-down winner. It was the first time that the defences were allowed to drop, and he entertained us all that night with the story of his immigration to Canada.

It seems that in his eagerness to adapt to his new country, he frantically practised what smattering of English he could pick up on the boat, and was armed and ready for his assigned destination in Alberta. Five minutes on the street, however, had him convinced that somehow he had taken a wrong turn. The gibberish all around him was certainly not English! It was weeks before he could be made to understand that the little community of St. Paul was one of the few French-speaking towns in western Canada, and that he hadn't been led astray by some sadistic immigration official.

Too soon our little aerie above Eighth Avenue had to be vacated. We simply couldn't afford the rent increase to twenty dollars a month, so we packed up our cartoons and easels and moved out to the Coste House in Mount Royal to join the SAIT art students who had been relocated there for the duration of the war. While we lost that special sense of closeness, we found a new home and were part of a vital community of artists as the Coste House, under Archie Key's direction, became the Allied Arts Centre of Calgary.

Above: *The Coste House, where the Sketch Club relocated after the war, became the Allied Arts Centre of Calgary.*

Facing Page: *Janet Mitchell chats with Max Bates at a gathering of local artists in the conservatory of the Coste House.*

Decisions, Decisions

by Helen Jull

Helen (Steeves) Jull grew up in Calgary and after graduating from the University of Alberta worked at the Calgary Herald *until she could no longer afford the privilege. As she says, "My salary was sixty dollars a month and all the newsprint I could eat."*

Mrs. Jull currently operates a small business and mothers an assortment of children of different size, shape and sex. She invites all interested parties to contact their grand-

mother for verification of the children's talents, intelligence and beauty.

Canadian children, as she relates in her story, were very much caught up in the war effort during the early 1940s. School students were often awarded "promotions" to higher rank according to their contributions, and the National War Finance Committee encouraged this kind of competition.

I must have been about eight years old so I, of course, did not realize what they were doing to my classmates and to me. It was not until many years later, when I understood the mechanics of propaganda, that I realized we were being carefully taught to hate. Systematically and week by week, taught to hate.

In Earl Grey Elementary School and indeed other schools across Canada, War Savings Stamps were sold. Each week, I brought my twenty-five-cents allowance to school. I was then able to buy and stick a stamp on my little bingo-like card thus donating my bit to the war effort. As the European war darkened and deepened, Dad mounted a huge map of Europe on a light-weight sheet of metal which was kept behind the door at the top of the basement stairs. I loved going to get it for each evening's radio news broadcast because, if I rattled it just right, it sounded like thunder and scared the socks off my wire-haired terrier, Skippy.

After Pearl Harbor it must have been necessary to step up the sale of War Savings Stamps, so some creative genius devised the plan of making a picture with a sheet of lickable stamps to fit on a cardboard poster, ruled in the right-sized squares. One particularly memorable scene on the wall near my desk was of a sinking "Jap" submarine. The class had to start buying the blue water around the edges of the picture and, as the coffers filled, the stamps started to include bits of the railing, deck and conning tower of the listing sub in the flaming water.

Canadian school children waged heroic battles in team competitions for military-like promotions in aid of the war effort.

At the same time, we had been divided into teams according to rows and were frantically racing to buy sticky bits of uniforms, guns or other essential equipment for "our" serviceman. My team had an air force man which was appropriate since I had two older cousins (of whom I was very proud) who had been lost with the RCAF.

Innumerable Saturday afternoons, my brother and I and all our friends went to the movies at the Tivoli Theatre. They always included newsreels of planes being shot down, ships sinking and other edifying sights for the little children assembled there. I can still hear the roaring whine as a Zero or Messerschmitt fighter plane heeled over and plummeted, smoking and flaming to earth, always accompanied by the cheers, hoots and hollers from the kids. We were especially delighted when a "Nazi" or "Jap" plane exploded into a fireball in midair. The good guys versus bad guys neatly translated to real life for us eight year olds. Since the reality of war was so far removed we were too young to be aware that the cowboy movies and newsreels of real tragedy were far different genres.

I remember that each week we gathered around the radio in the evening and listened to the continuing dramatization of air force heroes in action. The Lancaster bombers and their crews were very real in my vivid young imagination. Each week I felt a surge of pride at the ringing words, "Bombs away!" Each week I felt panic when "our" starboard engine or rear gunner was hit by The Enemy. Each week I breathed a sigh of relief when the white cliffs and green fields of England were reported in sight over the crackling inter-com of the plane and knew, once again, we made it. I remember the rousing song "Coming in on a Wing and a Prayer" and find that my eyes still water when I think about "There'll be blue birds over the white cliffs of Dover, Tomorrow when the world is free."

One bright school morning I was faced with a critical decision. Would my twenty-five-cent stamp be used to furnish our airman with a vital piece of equipment, or to complete the Rising Sun insignia and thereby finish the sinking of the "Jap" sub? Classmate advocates called out for both plans of action. I was torn. Finally, in the truly bloodthirsty fashion of a typical third grader, I chose to complete the destruction of the sub.

Guilt lay heavily on me. I, Helen Steeves, personally, had let down the Royal Canadian Air Force! Somewhere, some gallant airman would not have *the* critical equipment he needed because of my missing twenty-five-cents. What raw emotions for a child.

I suppose it was essential for all little children to feel they were participating in the war in these ways. The alternatives would have been far worse. However, I am truly very grateful that I have not had to teach, and then try to un-teach, my children about "lost" cousins, The Enemy, and how to hate.

Farrow's Drug Store was headquarters for the "25 Club", and the girls pictured here patriotically enlisted new memberships. War stamps were priced so that even children could spend their allowance money, and thus "do their bit" for the boys overseas.

The Guide's Cup Race

by J. Fred Scott

Colonel J. Fred Scott was born in Ireland in 1892 but followed his brother who had emigrated to Canada. He enlisted as a soldier in the First World War in order to expedite becoming a lawyer and, according to plan, attended Osgoode Hall following his tour of duty. The military, however, had made a lasting impression on the young Calgary lawyer and he joined the peacetime cavalry. In 1935 he was awarded a medal by the King in commemoration of the Silver Jubilee, and when the Second World War broke out, Scott led the Sixth Infantry Brigade, battle training the Canadian contingent. For many years following the war, Colonel Scott led the Calgary Highlanders, and his memoirs, which are preserved in the archives of the Glenbow Museum in Calgary, read like a personal history of pioneer Calgary.

Sydney Turner, Colonel Scott's daughter, contributed this article in her father's memory. She writes: "This excerpt about the Guide's Cup Race is from my late father's memoirs. Although the advent of the Second World War ended the races, I can recall riding with him through the Sarcee Reserve as he went about preparing for the ordeal."

As a Cavalry man with two daughters, I soon had three saddle horses with a stall for two of them built into our garage in Mount Royal, and the third picketed across the road on a large undeveloped school park area. It was not long until these became top polo ponies. I had become second in command of the Fifteenth Light Horse Cavalry unit and the Guide's Cup Race became a target and an obsession.

This was a point to point race to cover fourteen miles, as the crow flies, and ran across the Sarcee Indian Reserve. Each rider had a time space of seven minutes. It became a contest of general horsemanship and map reading. It was laid out with seven legs, and the first direction card merely gave a distance (of about two miles) and the direction. In a very rugged country it was up to the rider to decide how to arrive at the first destination. There he had to negotiate a four-foot six-inch jump, and then take a card to find which way to go for his second leg. Thus it continued from point to point. To find these points was a tricky business because the country was quite heavily wooded, and it was only by using the cattle trails which were marked on the map that one could hope to be successful. On one occasion, I was the winner with Brigadier Fred

Harvey, V.C. We tied in a time of one hour and thirty minutes, having covered eighteen miles. At the termination of the race, the horse then had to eat a pound and a half of oats or be disqualified.

I have been in the race three times, and I have seen three horses killed and two riders very seriously injured. It was a contest open to Permanent Force Officers and Militia Officers, providing such officer owned his own mount, and it was run alternately at Petawawa for Eastern Canada and at Sarcee for the West.

Real Estate in the Good Ol' Bad Ol' Days

by Frank Johns

Frank Johns, FRI, entered the business of real estate in 1936 in Toronto. He is the past president of the Calgary Real Estate Board and first honorary life member of the Alberta Real Estate Association. In 1969 he was president of the Canadian Institute of Realtors. In addition to his various business-related associations, Mr. Johns has also been very active in his community as president of the Downtown Kiwanis Club, as a member of numerous Calgary City Council committees, and as a board member of the Grace Hospital, Mount Royal College and the Salvation Army.

During the Depression of the 1930s, Calgary saw very little increase in population and a minimum amount of house building and general construction. All this changed with the outbreak of the Second World War. A great many Canadians volunteered, others were conscripted for military service, and this dramatically reduced the amount of unemployment across the country.

When it became obvious that the war would not be over as quickly as many had originally predicted, and that the Allies were in for a long fight, Canada was chosen as the site for the training of air crew under the British Commonwealth Air Training Plan. Many Air Force units were established on the prairies, several of which were in or around Calgary, in addition to the Canadian Navy and Army bases.

As the enlisted personnel were posted to Calgary and district for training, many brought along their families to be with them for the period prior to their transfers overseas. Since there had been very little house construction during the years immediately before the outbreak of hostilities, there was suddenly a shortage of rental accommodation. It was necessary for the Federal Government to introduce rent controls in an effort to ensure that those in uniform, as well as others in essential industry, were not taken advantage of as a result of the national emergency.

During the 1940s, with literally thousands of people coming to Calgary to accept employment or to undergo military training, the role of real estate men became rather important. There were very few large real estate companies. Real estate was almost a corner grocery store type opera-

From the arrival of the CPR, real estate has been big business in Calgary, and this false-fronted office looked out expectantly in 1907 over the yet-barren prairie of the north hill.

tion, with an agent selling or renting real estate and insurance from a small neighbourhood office. Houses sold for as little as five hundred dollars, and a five thousand dollar sale was a fairly good-sized transaction. While today buyers and investors in real estate are much more sophisticated and understand the necessity of various forms of financing, back in the '40s buyers were somewhat frightened of the term "mortgage" and the long-term commitment it involved. Many of them had visions of "Simon Legree" and fears of getting into the clutches of the mortgagee.

When the war ended, Calgary, along with other major cities across Canada, entered a boom period. The Federal Government brought in the National Housing Act, with interest rates of four-and-a-half percent, to enable people to purchase their own homes. At the same time they hoped to stimulate the house building industry which would give employment to many returning servicemen. There was a pent-up demand for many items which were not obtainable during the war years, and many Canadians had built up fairly healthy savings accounts which they could now invest in housing. At the same time, many young veterans, who before the war had lived in the country, decided, because of job opportunities or the desire for a different life style, to live in the metropolitan areas. So, from a population of just eighty-five thousand at the end of the Second World War, Calgary continued to grow, and this trend was accelerated in the following

Niblock and Tull operated a three man, one-room real estate office in 1909, ready to promote the city's sky's-the-limit possibilities.

years as a result of the development of the petroleum industry. The "Stampede City" became the administrative headquarters for the "Oil Patch".

I know that progress and change are inevitable and, while I sometimes look back to the old days with nostalgia, I know they will not return. The practice of real estate today is in many ways more professional and more organized, but it has lost some of its personalized service.

Today the real estate agent drives his clients to view prospective new homes. In the '40s, however, as a result of wartime demands, a number of consumer items were restricted. Of importance to real estate sales people was the rationing of gasoline. In spite of the nature of their work they received exactly the same number of gasoline coupons as any other citizen. And, since Calgary's public transport system serviced the city by a collection of streetcars, it was not uncommon for a real estate person, once he had determined what the customer and his wife wanted and could afford, to present them with a map — tell them what route to take, — and then hand over streetcar tickets so they could go and view the property by themselves.

And oh yes, — if the prospects looked like serious buyers — with a capacity to rent or purchase, they would then be given *extra* tickets so that they could come back to the office and write up an offer. Those were the days!

201

Dr. Milne was a scholar of the old school who believed that honest labour was a prescription for most of society's ills. He supported himself through medical school selling barbed wire to western homesteaders.

The Doctors

by Keir MacGougan

Dr. Keir MacGougan was born in Summerside, Prince Edward Island in 1907, and was educated in the Maritimes. He received his medical degree from McGill University in 1935, and took his Eye, Ear, Nose and Throat Speciality at Montreal General Hospital. Following service during the Second World War, Dr. MacGougan came to Calgary to set up his practice.

No doctor likes to talk about the patients he lost, but Dr. MacGougan still gleefully tells about the one that got away. It seems the unfortunate victim of this particular tale had inhaled a peanut into his lung. Though the operating room was tiny, the floor slippery and the table wobbly, the Doctor immediately performed a bronchoscopy. Out popped the peanut in Dr. MacGougan's death-like clutch. However, in the tension of the moment the surgeon's feet slipped out from under him, knocking the table off its precarious perch, and the patient flew skidding out the operating door into the hospital corridor. Both eventually recovered.

The social centre for all the news, rumours and tall tales of the medical community in Calgary was the Doctor's Room of the hospital. It was there that we young practitioners got sage advice from Dr. Frank Wilson about the stock market, and were offered cheap oil shares — guaranteed to double in value daily — by Dr. Beauchemin. We could afford neither the advice nor the stocks, so we stayed as poor and overworked as ever, but our time spent there gave us a wealth of medical legends.

Dr. Milne was a scholar of the old school who believed that honest labour was a prescription for most of society's ills. He had supported himself through medical school selling barbed wire to western homesteaders. His practice in Trochu ended at the outbreak of the First World War when he went to England to do a Fellowship in Surgery, and his army commission kept him in London until the end of the conflict. When he returned he was offered a position at the Mayo Clinic but turned it down to settle again in his beloved West, and soon he established a practice in Calgary. Thorough and fussy, giving excellent care to his patients, he was nonetheless not anxious to have his personal life intruded upon.

The medical community had struggled along with the rest of Alberta's population through the Depression years, and was alarmed by the economic theories of Mr. Aberhart's Social Credit. Hospital corridors buzzed with talk of the upcoming election in 1935 and everyone wanted to know how Dr. Milne would vote. No amount of subtle urging would elicit any kind of political opinion, so finally one colleague asked him straight out, "Well, how *are* you going to vote?" There was considerable delay while Dr. Milne pondered the question. Finally he replied, "By secret ballot."

Dr. Noel Smith was a somewhat more irrepressible gentleman who had emigrated to Calgary from Ireland following the Second World War. He joined a clinic for a number of years so it was not until quite far along into his career that he got a taste of private practice. Very quickly he became renowned for his house calls.

Smith liked to get things done in a hurry and had little patience for the malingerer. Unfortunately, one lady hypochondriac, underestimating his attention to duty, decided that maybe she could slip away from her sick bed for an irresistible hour of shopping before the doctor's anticipated house call. The hour stretched to two and Dr. Smith arrived, as scheduled, at the door. Each stab at the bell raised his blood pressure until finally, rage knowing no bounds, he kicked the door off its hinges!

The demolition calmed him considerably, so he paused long enough to leave his patient a note which he tacked to the remains. "I assumed when you didn't respond to the doorbell that your illness had become critical, and in my haste to attend to your crisis I fear I might have damaged your door."

It is not reported whether the lady ever required further medical attention from Dr. Smith.

Nick Bidniak

by Illingworth Kerr

Illingworth H. Kerr was born in 1905 in Saskatchewan. He received some guidance from his mother, an amateur water colourist, but it wasn't until after high school that he went to Toronto, with a hundred dollars in his pocket, to attend an art course at the Central Technical School. From there he entered the Ontario College of Art where he studied under Arthur Lismer, J.E.H MacDonald, F.H. Varley and J.W. Beatty. He wrote: "Fortunately a childless uncle staked me when the need arose."

In 1928 he returned to Saskatchewan and established a studio above the Lumsden Poolhall. "My canvases were usually based on field sketches done at every opportunity – while trapping and moose hunting in northern Saskatchewan, while sign painting on the prairie or while harvesting."

These experiences, in addition to the drought and Depression, made him eager to look farther afield, so he went to Europe as a cattlehand on a cargo boat where he studied at the Westminister School of Art in London. To help support himself he wrote stories about Canada for Blackwood's Magazine and painted dioramas of Canadian life for the Glasgow Empire Exhibition.

He returned to Canada in 1939, and by 1947 was appointed Art Director at the Provincial Institute of Technology and Art in Calgary. His works are represented in the permanent collections of many galleries and museums, including the Glenbow Museum, Calgary, and the National Gallery of Canada.

Today it is the Alberta College of Art. In post-war days it was merely the Art Department of the Provincial Institute of Technology and Art (SAIT today) and we were eager to expand our small student body. No one was turned away, not even a young Greek who had complete lack of English. Still, it *was* shocking to find that one would-be applicant had only one eye and no arms. For a career in art? Pas possible!

Nick Bidniak, of Ukrainian parentage, was born in Toronto. At age three, however, he was sent to Russia where he was raised by an uncle and aunt. The war broke out and Nick's family was working as enforced labour at a German prison camp when, in a turnip field, at age sixteen, Nick encountered a land mine. Somehow it failed to kill him.

Nick, being born Canadian, was allowed entry to Canada and came to us under the auspices of the Ukrainians at Vegreville. He proved to be handsome, exceedingly polite, and was rapidly learning English. Many wonderful Ukrainian students we had, but never one like Nick.

Handicapped artists usually use their feet or teeth in lieu of hands. Nick Bidniak had a method of his own. He worked without a jacket. To the stub of his right arm, using his teeth, he would attach a two or three inch heavy elastic made from an automobile inner tube. Into this powerful non-skid band he would insert a pencil, a brush, or whatever tool he needed. His equipment he plucked from a breast pocket with his strong white teeth.

Now the miracle: he drew or painted with a shoulder movement so that his whole body seemed to power itself into the action! His lines and tonalities were as sensitive, and often more so, than the work of his fellow students.

Desiring to check a perspective course given to our first year students by the Drafting Department, I took the course myself. I elected to have the drafting desk next to Nick's so that I could render aid. We simply could not conceive of him using rulers, set squares and compasses, but I was amazed to find that, after the first few sessions, I was completely unaware of Nick because he always found a way to accomplish the assigned projects without assistance from anyone.

In a time that was excitedly aware of cubism, surrealism and various kinds of expressionism, it was hard to direct Nick's painting. He was deep into Byzantine symbolism and demanded instruction in glazing, an outmoded technique. When most painters were substituting colour shapes for modelled form, Nick wanted balloonlike volumes.

This peaked in a third year Commercial Drawing class when I set some projects in fashion illustration, wherein the models were required to appear elegantly slim, "eight heads tall, not the usual six." Nick's ladies always looked like well-padded peasants. I protested. So did Nick. "But women aren't like that!" he shouted. "Women aren't like that!"

Nick never adjusted to the vulgar standards of American advertising but such was the fantastic ingenuity of this armless, one-eyed young man that we had ceased to regard him as handicapped. However, we were always painfully aware of it at year's end when our annual exhibition of student work was held. Very proud we were of a great array of drawings, paintings, sculpture, ceramics, and commercial projects done in our various courses. Surely the newspaper reporters would give us that much-desired publicity which would boost our enrollment. But did they? No; they had heard of our armless wonder and for four years just one student out of two hundred caught all the limelight.

Calgary Circa 1948

by Susan MacLeod

Susan (Longshore) MacLeod arrived in Calgary along with her father Willard Longshore who was transferred from Wyoming as head of the Land Department of Stanolind Oil and Gas. He was the first employee of the Canadian Division as well as its first retiree, and was founder and first president of the Alberta Landmen's Association.

Susan and her brother and sister received care packages from their American grandmothers on their first Canadian Christmas, filled with stocking caps and Hershey Bars and Life Saver Books. "It wasn't long though, before future Christmases brought Canadian gifts into our lives: skis and toboggans and toques and parkas; bone china teacups for our mother and mysterious gifts wrapped in royal-purple-flannel drawstring bags for Father."

I was twelve years old when my dad was transferred to Calgary. He was part of that huge migration of American oil men following the discovery of the Leduc field, and we arrived in Alberta rather dumbfounded by the changes we faced.

Landing at the small green quonset-type airport building at McCall Field hardly prepared us for our temporary quarters in the Palliser Hotel. We really didn't think ourselves grand enough to be housed in such opulence, but accommodation was so scarce in those post-war years that we were captive, a least for a little while, in that magnificent grey castle. There were wide-flowing staircases and glittering chandeliers, and attendants to ride us up and down in the elevators, and, just to acclimate us, a freezing February wind that whipped our breath away when we ventured out to explore the new city.

Finally we found a house. I remember it as huge and drafty, with a milk chute by the back door. An open, horse-drawn wagon delivered the glass milk bottles and we gaped with wonder at the cardboard-covered, ice-cream-cone caps perched precariously like hats on snowmen.

My bedroom upstairs had a very cold hardwood floor with an attached screened summer-porch. It had a gas heater fireplace and blue and white wallpaper which eternally bloomed pink roses. The connecting door led to my brother's room, but I sealed off the alcove with the cardtable I set up where I did my homework each night.

We walked along the river path to get to school and had to make the choice anew each

Like the children pictured here, we walked along the river path to get to school, and had to make the choice anew each day: which bridge would we cross? The swinging bridge was a wire and rope affair, which swayed and swung with each footfall, and was to be avoided at all costs if boys *were on it.*

day: which bridge would we cross? The swinging bridge was a wire and rope affair which swayed and swung with each footfall and was to be avoided at all costs if *boys* were on it. *Their* favorite sport seemed to be swinging the bridge by shifting their weight from side to side, whooping and hollering, while *our* only avenue of escape was the yawning chasm of space and the icy river below. Infinitely to be preferred was the Mission Bridge — a sturdy stone and cement traffic bridge — close by a cluster of convenience stores which provided us with Cherry Blossoms and Sweet Maries and other after-school treats. If we walked along that route we passed by Whitburn's Greenhouses and the wonderful tropical greens growing beneath the glass roofs.

How odd it seemed to crunch along through the icy streets only inches from that indoor jungle. One day, however, my sister left for school a few minutes early, only to come rushing back with the exciting announcement, "Hey! Guess what! We have a sidewalk!" We all rushed outdoors to be greeted by the warm soft breeze that signaled the arrival of our first chinook. Miraculously, as we slept, the sidewalk snow had melted and Elbow Drive was awash in slush. We were having a reprieve!

Index of Authors

Photo Credits

Photographs from Glenbow Archives

p. 16	NA - 2204 - 8	p. 75	NA - 4100 - 8	pp. 138-139	NA - 2193 - 7
pp. 16-17	NA - 1035 - 3	pp. 78-79	NA - 4019 - 9	p. 141 *upper*	NC - 24 - 38
p. 18 *upper*	NA - 541 - 1	p. 81	NA - 3303 - 1	*lower*	NA - 2517 - 3
lower	NA - 1315 - 4	p. 82 *upper*	NA - 446 - 132	p. 145	NA - 1616 - 1
p. 19	NA - 1315 - 6	*lower*	NA - 1178 - 2	p. 147	NA - 3334 - 13
pp. 20-21	NA - 1315 - 7	p. 84	ND - 10 - 11	p. 149	NA - 2800 - 12
p. 23	NA - 2450 - 1	p. 85	NC - 24 - 31	p. 150	NA - 4355 - 15
p. 26	NA - 468 - 13	p. 87	NA - 3752 - 30	p. 155 *upper*	ND - 10 - 55
p. 27	NA - 468 - 12	p. 88 *upper*	NA - 3026 - 21	*lower*	ND - 10 - 96
pp. 28-29	NA - 81 - 7	*lower*	NA - 2316 - 7	p. 158	NA - 2891 - 15
p. 30 *left*	NA - 3186 - 1	p. 89 *upper*	NA - 924 - 1	p. 160	ND - 10 - 179
	NA - 3186 - 2	*lower*	NA - 2553 - 4	p. 162	ND - 10 - 19
p. 31	NC - 26 - 27	p. 90	NA - 1258 - 22	p. 165	NA - 2771 - 2
pp. 32-33	NA - 2575 - 4	p. 91	NA - 3691 - 32	p. 167	ND - 10 - 2
p. 35	NA - 1390 - 2	p. 92 *upper*	NA - 3247	p. 168	NA - 2037 - 21
p. 36	NA - 250 - 3	*lower*	NA - 334 - 15	p. 169	NA - 1119 - 8
p. 39	NA - 3985 - 24	p. 93	NA - 3277 - 54	p. 173	NB - 16 - 424
p. 41	NA - 583 - 1	p. 95	NA - 1898 - 2	p. 175	NA - 1635 - 2
p. 42	NA - 468 - 15	pp. 98-99	NA - 1604 - 57	p. 177 *upper*	NA - 3668 - 19
pp. 42-43	NA - 395 - 15	p. 99	NA - 3984 - 6	*lower*	NA - 3668 - 9
p. 45 *upper*	NA - 1372 - 3	p. 102	NA - 67 - 132	p. 178	NA - 2901 - 12
lower	NA - 3096 - 1	p. 103	NA - 711 - 8	p. 180	NA - 2901 - 5
pp. 46-47	NA - 3589 - 14	pp. 104-105	NA - 67 - 67	p. 181	NA - 1655 - 1
p. 49	NA - 667 - 428	p. 108	NA - 2831 - 6	p. 183	NA - 373 - 1
p. 50	NA - 1241 - 847	p. 110	NA - 1266 - 1	p. 184	NA - 3965 - 15
p. 52	NA - 1105 - 8	p. 113 *upper*	NA - 1604 - 38	p. 186	NA - 3965 - 16
p. 54	NA - 468 - 6	*lower*	ND - 10 - 3	pp. 188-189	NA - 3316 - 72
p. 55	NA - 1586 - 6	p. 114	NA - 2365 - 22	p. 190	NA - 3316 - 69
p. 57	NA - 667 - 285	p. 116	NA - 2922 - 4	p. 191	P - 1583 - 32
pp. 58-59	NA - 1604 - 35	p. 122	NA - 609 - 1	p. 192	NA - 3562 - 16
p. 60	NA - 963 - 1	p. 125	NA - 3092 - 89	p. 193	NA - 1735 - 1
p. 62	NA - 3627 - 40	p. 126	NA - 4035 - 91	p. 196	NA - 2864 - 3436
p. 64	NA - 1641 - 1	p. 128	NC - 26 - 152	p. 200	NA - 2922 - 5
p. 70	NA - 2036 - 3	p. 131	NA - 2159 - 9	p. 201	NA - 2077 - 9
p. 71	NA - 3884 - 8	p. 132	NA - 3885 - 34	p. 202	NA - 3202 - 1
p. 73	NA - 2732 - 3	p. 138	NA - 3971 - 3		

Photographs from Other Sources

p. 48	Mrs. A. Thorpe
p. 66	Mrs. M. Burns
p. 101	Calgary Herald
p. 119	Miss Janet Mitchell
p. 123	Miss Allison Jackson
p. 133	Calgary Zoological Society
p. 134	Mrs. Warren Stewart
p. 143	Mr. A.R. Smith
p. 148	Mr. G. Cummings
p. 152	Mrs. Patricia Pryde
p. 195	The Calgary Herald
p. 208	Mrs. Susie Sparks

Author Photographs

All biographical photographs are courtesy of Crowchild Photographic Ltd., excepting those supplied by individual authors:

Allan Anderson	M.M. Porter
Hugh Dempsey	Eva Reid
Ruth Gorman	Ruth Rothel
Don Harvie	Jack Saucier
Anele Jenkins	Grace Shaw
Keir MacGougan	Art Smith
Janet Mitchell	Joan Weir
Tom Moore	

Index